LATINO
TALENT

LATINO TALENT

EFFECTIVE STRATEGIES
TO RECRUIT, RETAIN, AND DEVELOP
HISPANIC PROFESSIONALS

ROBERT RODRIGUEZ, PhD

John Wiley & Sons, Inc.

For general information on our other products and services or for technical support, please contact our Customer Care Department within the United States at (800) 762-2974, outside the United States at (317) 572-3993 or fax (317) 572-4002.

Wiley also publishes its books in a variety of electronic formats. Some content that appears in print may not be available in electronic books. For more information about Wiley products, visit our web site at www.wiley.com.

ISBN-13: 978-0-470-12523-6

Printed in the United States of America.

10 9 8 7 6 5 4 3 2 1

In loving memory of my grandmother,
Guadalupe Rodriguez

CONTENTS

LIST OF TABLES AND FIGURES

PREFACE

I have two goals for writing this book. First, I want to provide information that will give organizational leaders a deeper, broader understanding of Latinos and their culture. Without this knowledge, non-Latinos may be confused and misunderstand Latino behaviors and attitudes that are reflective of that culture. The insights gained from reading this book will help you recognize when cultural differences may be the root cause of problems experienced within a workforce that has an increasing Latino population. After reading this book, you will be better able to see the workplace as Latinos see it, providing the foundation for building crucial bridges of understanding. The rapid growth in the U.S. Latino population along with their rising purchasing power provides a significant business incentive for acquiring this understanding. In addition to being good for business, this understanding has a positive impact on our society as a whole. This book was written for business leaders, human resource executives, diversity practitioners, and managers—the people who are often charged with creating inclusive work environments and developing talent management initiatives.

The second goal is to enhance the experience of Latinos in the workplace so that they feel validated, appreciated, heard, and accepted. This became a goal after I completed the book as a result of the personal growth I experienced in the process of writing it. As I gathered information and read what others had said about similar topics, I learned a great deal more about what it meant to be Latino.

It is my sincere hope that the Latinos who read this book, by reading more about their heritage and cultural values, will be better able to validate and integrate their unique identity. This group faces a large amount of pressure in defining themselves in a society that often criticizes their identity and seeks to impose definitions rather than allow for self-identification (Ferdman and Gallegos, 2001). Sadly, many of us know precious little about ourselves and our history. Without this insight, Latinos may not be able to look inward at their role in and contribution to situations in which they find themselves. The information presented in this book will help Latinos develop an understanding of and sensitivity to the nuances of their cultural heritage.

The book takes a rather straightforward approach. Chapter 1 provides an analysis of two critical areas, knowledge capital and purchasing power, and how Latinos are impacting these areas more significantly each day. This chapter reinforces the idea that knowledge capital and purchasing power provide a business incentive for investing time and money in the talent management initiatives highlighted throughout the book. Also included in this chapter are insights about the Latino consumer market that organizations can use to tap into this growing segment of the marketplace.

In Chapter 2, the focus moves toward educating readers about the Latino population from both a qualitative and quantitative perspective. Qualitatively, Chapter 2 explores the terminology most associated with the Latino community. By understanding these terms, organizational leaders are better able to describe and understand Latino diversity. Quantitatively, the L15 concept is introduced, referring to the 15 fundamental metrics about the Latino community that those involved in Latino initiatives need to know. These 15 metrics convincingly argue that organizations need to raise their level of urgency regarding Latino-related initiatives.

Chapter 3 describes the cultural and ethnic aspects of the Latino community. Here the focus is on the cultural elements that not only unite Latinos, but also explains how these cultural elements differentiate Latinos from non-Latinos. In this chapter, you gain an understanding of how Latinos view the world and interact with others.

In Chapters 4, 5, and 6, the focus shifts to an emphasis on providing practical solutions and strategies associated with Latino talent management programs. These strategies are better understood because of the foundation that was laid in Chapters 1, 2, and 3.

Chapter 4 explains 21 techniques that companies can apply immediately to improve the recruitment of Latino professionals. This chapter also highlights common mistakes made by organizations when recruiting Latinos and stresses the importance of creating a positive employment brand within the Latino community.

Chapter 5 looks at strategies that companies can promote to help raise the level of performance and the retention of Latino employees. Case studies emphasize the best practices top organizations use to improve Latino employee retention.

Chapter 6 provides learning and development recommendations that are geared toward Latino employees and their managers. Because of elements unique to Latino heritage, programs aimed at promoting personal and professional growth of Latino employees need to be unique as well and this chapter highlights why.

Chapter 7 looks toward the future and highlights the role that companies can play in promoting a workplace and society that is more inclusive to Latinos for the benefit of everyone. Specifically, we look at what needs to be done to help create a pipeline of future Latino leaders and what must be done to raise the level of educational attainment within the Latino community. Both of these areas influence the future impact that Latinos will have on the U.S. workplace. Also addressed is the need for more research regarding talent management strategies. It is important for employers to create a vision for the future that includes better integration of the Latino workforce.

Chapter 8 connects directly with Latino readers. I share my experience as a son of migrant workers who has been able to achieve some level of academic and professional success. My struggles with my cultural heritage will undoubtedly mirror the experience of some of my Latino readers. In this chapter, I offer advice to fellow Latinos on how they can leverage their "Latino-ness" as an asset.

At the end of the book, an Appendix lists Latino organizations and associations that can be useful for organizations and Latinos alike. For additional insights about how companies are leveraging the key messages that are shared in this book, go to www. latinotalentbook. com.

Last, let me leave you with some final observations about the book. First, I chose to use the term *Latino* instead of *Hispanic* to refer to this ethnic community. Chapter 2 provides some insight into the debate within the community regarding the terms Latino and Hispanic. I prefer the word Latino and I use it generically to refer to both genders to avoid having to repeatedly say Latinos and Latinas when referencing to members of this ethnic community.

Second, I want to remind readers that individual members of the Latino community vary widely with how closely they relate to the Latino archetype. Some Latinos will closely mirror some of the ethnic characteristics I use in the book to describe the community while others might not share any of the Latino cultural attributes. The presence or absence of these characteristics in any one Latino are not as important as the interconnectedness these attributes have in defining one's sense of identity. I share these cultural differences so that they can be appreciated and understood by others—not to encourage stereotyping, prejudice, and discrimination. Every individual has the right to be treated as a unique individual but that should not prevent us from looking at the general characteristics of an ethnic group to better understand who they are.

Acknowledgments

The completion of this book would not have been possible without the support, encouragement, and inspiration of my family and friends. First, I express gratitude to my colleagues at Kaplan University, particularly Dr. Eric Goodman, for allowing me the time to research and write this book, and for trusting me to lead Kaplan's Latino-related initiatives. I thank my friends at the Hispanic Alliance for Career Enhancement (HACE), who provided the inspiration for writing this book by all that they are doing to build and nurture the careers of Latino professionals. Special thanks to Abe Tomás Hughes, HACE's former president and CEO, for providing an excellent example of organizational leadership and for pushing me to grow personally and professionally.

I'd also like to thank those who preceded me in writing about the Latino experience in the workplace, including Dr. Norma Carr-Ruffino whose book on managing diversity helped to show me the power of creating an inclusive work environment. To Nilda Chong and Francia Baez, authors of the book *Latino Culture,* goes my gratitude for helping me learn about what it means to be a Latino and for providing the foundation for my book.

I extend my utmost respect and appreciation to my fellow academics Drs. Marta Elvira and Bernardo Ferdman for helping me develop my scholarly voice and for teaching me about the importance of Latino identity. To Raymond Arroyo at Aetna, Rosie Saez at Wachovia, and Isaias Zamarripa at General Mills—thank you for being such wonderful role models and for sharing the wonderful work you are doing at your organizations.

To my mom and dad, German and Janie Olivarez, thank you for instilling in me a passion for learning at such a young age and for being such loving parents. To my two amazing young sons, Bailey and Benjamin, I hope this book helps you gain an even broader sense of the richness of the Latino heritage and that you'll use this insight as you progress on your journey to becoming the next generation of Latino leaders. May your voices always be heard and valued.

And to my amazing wife Lisa, my heartfelt appreciation for the patience and loving support you provided me during the process of writing this book. This book is dedicated to you. Thank you for being a part of my life. I love you dearly.

AUTHOR BIOGRAPHY

Robert Rodriguez, PhD, is the chairman of the board of directors for the Hispanic Alliance for Career Enhancement (HACE), a leading national nonprofit organization dedicated to building Latino careers through leadership and development of Latino students and experienced professionals. He has consulted for several leading corporations on their Latino talent strategy including Abbott Labs, Supervalu, Wachovia, DaimlerChrysler, Darden Restaurants, and Allianz Life. He also serves as the assistant dean of the Graduate School of Management at Kaplan University and is in charge of their Latino educational initiatives. Prior to academia, Dr. Rodriguez held human resource leadership roles at 3M, Amoco, and R.R. Donnelley & Sons. He has published over 25 articles on a variety of diversity and human resource strategy topics and is a frequent speaker at national human resource and diversity conferences. Dr. Rodriguez is the son of immigrant parents from Mexico who used the passion for learning instilled in him by his parents to become the first member of his extended family to attend college. He earned his bachelors degree in business management in 1991, his masters degree in human resource management in 1996, and his PhD in organization development in 2001. He is also a graduate of the UCLA Latino Leadership Institute. In 2006, the Hispanic Chamber of Commerce of Minnesota recognized Dr. Rodriguez as a leading Latino leader under the age of 40. Robert and his family reside in Chicago, Illinois.

For more information about the author and his work with leading corporations regarding Latino talent initiatives, go to www.latinotalentbook.com.

LATINO TALENT

CHAPTER 1

THE BUSINESS CASE FOR LATINO DIVERSITY

The trend is clear and the ramifications are obvious: the Latino community in the United States is having a tremendous impact on society in general and on the American labor force in particular. Demographic shifts in the coming years will only increase the significance of this group, making the U.S. Latino community difficult to ignore. Already it is almost impossible to go a day without seeing the influence Latinos wield. You see it through their emerging political, demographic, and economic impact. Latinos will continue to have a profound impact on society, culture, relationships, consumerism, the workforce, the economy, and business. For example, according to the Hispanic/Latino Market Profile report published by the Magazine Publishers of America (2004, p. 9), 80 percent of the teen population in Los Angeles is Latino. Such a high concentration of young Latinos is having a huge impact on local government officials, school administrators, universities, and businesses.

Because human resource and diversity practitioners are often charged with crafting inclusive talent management strategies for their organizations, they need to take special notice of the growing Latino influence. Not just because the workplace of the near future will have an increasingly Latino identity, but because effective talent management programs need to be aligned with business strategies. Due to their growing population and subsequent rise in purchasing power, the Latino community is being incorporated into the business strategy of more and more organizations. This is partly why organizations looking to proactively leverage this community are raising the sense of urgency regarding their Latino talent management initiatives. Specifically, organizations are looking at Latinos to be their next great source of intellectual capital and to drive future revenue growth. As this chapter indicates, organizations that fail to develop strategies to better prepare themselves for this Latino wave run the risk of shrinking corporate profits and missing out on a huge pool of available talent.

SOURCE OF INTELLECTUAL CAPITAL

Much of the economic growth in the United States for the past 25 years has been due to the accumulation of knowledge. Today, close to 60 percent of the U.S. labor force consists of knowledge workers. As a result, the United States is one of the world leaders in technological advances, scientific discoveries, and innovation. However, demographic shifts in the U.S. labor force threaten to weaken America's global leadership position. If the United States is not able to sustain the talent pool required to support their knowledge economy, it will suffer a tremendous loss in intellectual and political power.

The Bureau of Labor statistics project that by 2008 two employees will be leaving the U.S. workforce for every new one entering. Even with the tremendous increases in productivity, this trend will cause a labor shortage of approximately 10 million employees for U.S. organizations in the near future. Historically, the 20-to-64 age group has been considered the primary source for the U.S. labor force. The U.S. economy has prospered and profited from strong growth in the 20-to-64 age group since 1970. However, beginning in 2010, Figure 1.1 indicates that growth in the 65-and-over

Figure 1.1
Change in Workforce and Retired Age Group

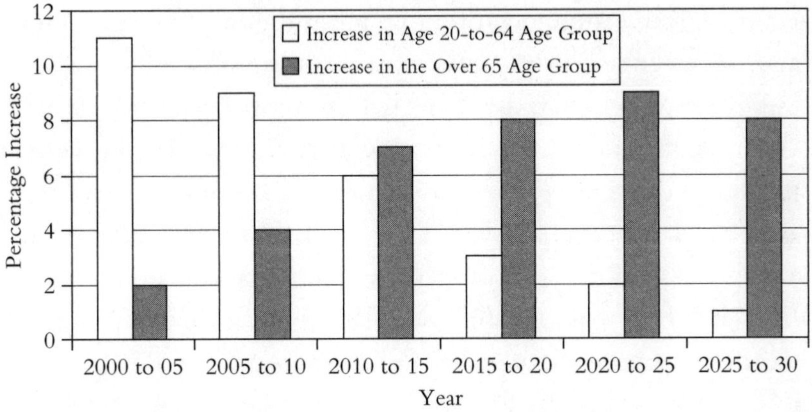

Source: Social Security Administration

age group will increase at a faster rate than the 20-to-64 age group. Between the years 2015 and 2020, the 65-and-over age group will increase at a rate twice that of the 20-to-64 age group. A bigger concern is that between 2020 and 2025, the 65-and-over age group will increase at a rate four times that of the 20-to-64 age group. If widespread labor shortages materialize, there may be dire consequences for the U.S. economy.

The driving force behind this pending labor shortage is the retirement of the baby-boom generation. The 76 million baby boomers were born post World War II from the years 1946 to 1964. This generation is beginning to hit retirement age and it is estimated that 10,000 baby boomers will be retiring every day over the next two decades (Retirement Living Information Center, 2004). As these baby boomers retire in increasing numbers, organizations will need a source of labor to fill the positions they have vacated. Increasingly, organizations are investigating their workforce demographics in an attempt to better understand the expected effects of the baby-boom exit. Some organizations are already outsourcing some of their work to meet their labor force needs but this is not a sustainable long-term solution for the United States for a variety of reasons. Clearly, those organizations able to prepare for the coming labor shortage will have a competitive advantage.

As baby boomers retire, they will be replaced by people who have a significantly different work experience. As this shortage of qualified, educated workers mounts, U.S. organizations will need to be much more responsive to the needs and expectations of the available labor force. As companies realize that the labor force of the near future will include a large percentage of Latinos, they are becoming increasingly interested in recruiting talented Latino candidates to fill managerial positions. Latino leaders who understand and can more effectively interact with Latino employees provide a partial solution to the pending labor shortage.

According to the Pew Hispanic Center, the rate of growth in the Latino labor force exceeds that of any other group in the United States. The *Latino Labor Report* indicates that Latinos are the only group in the current U.S. labor market that continues to grow in a substantial way. In fact, Latinos comprise a significant component of the new workers entering the labor force. Consider, for example, that between the second quarter of 2005 and the second quarter of 2006 the overall labor force grew by 2.1 million. Of those, 867,000 workers, or about 40 percent, were Latino (Kochhar, 2006).

Since Latinos will make up close to 25 percent of the workforce in the near future, understanding Latino communication styles and behavioral tendencies becomes increasingly essential as they move into supervisory and managerial positions in greater numbers (Chong and Baez, 2005). The war for top Latino talent is already intensifying as businesses across the United States are aggressively seeking Latino professionals to staff key positions. This can be seen through the proliferation of Latino job fairs, Latino online job boards, and the growing number of companies partnering with Latino nonprofit organizations, such as the Hispanic Alliance for Career Enhancement (HACE), to help enhance the effectiveness of Latino recruiting programs.

However, those employers who fail to appreciate and embrace the valuable cultural aspects that Latinos bring to the workplace run the risk of low productivity, employee dissatisfaction, lack of commitment, and turnover (Carr-Ruffino, 2003). Companies wishing to gain a competitive advantage should seek to better understand and enhance the experience of members of the Latino community in their workplace. Employers should also try to identify how their company culture influences the behavior and experience of Latinos (Ferdman and Cortes, 1992). Top Latino professionals, knowing that they are highly sought after, will become more selective and will only join organizations who recognize their individual and group needs and who make them feel appreciated and supported (Carr-Ruffino, 2003).

Latinos already have the highest rate of employment of any U.S. minority group and their role in the U.S. labor force will be even more prominent in the next few years. Human resource and diversity practitioners who see Latino diversity as exclusively a moral imperative are lacking a big picture perspective. To truly win the favor of senior management and to gain access to budget resources, Latino diversity needs to be viewed as a competitive advantage and business opportunity by those charged with leading Latino talent management initiatives.

LATINO PURCHASING POWER

If companies disregard the data on Latino demographics, they also disregard the substantial growth in the purchasing power of the Latino market. As companies search for new markets to help drive sales growth, they increasingly are setting their sights on the Latino community in an effort to attract new consumers. The Latino consumer market for 2007 is estimated at $800 billion. This size makes the U.S. Latino consumer market one of the top 10 largest economies in the world surpassing the gross national product (GNP) of entire countries including India, Mexico, Brazil, and Australia. Projections indicate that Latino purchasing power will soon surpass African American purchasing power in the United States and could reach $1 trillion by 2010. Besides pure population growth, some of the trends driving the growth in Latino purchasing power include increased Latino employment rates and the increased ability to receive credit.

One study indicates that since 1990 the Latino population in the United States has grown by 188 percent. However, during that same time, their purchasing power grew by 415 percent (Humphreys, 2006). In North Carolina, for example, Latino purchasing power has grown by over 1000 percent since 1990. Add to this the fact that Latinos have one of the highest percentages of disposable incomes of any minority group and you can clearly see the attractiveness of this market.

With such statistics, it is easy to see why Latino consumers are gaining the attention of businesses. They see the Latino market as a catalyst for economic growth. Successfully engaging the Latino market is no longer an option for businesses, it is quickly becoming the key to economic survival. According to a study conducted by HispanTelligence (2006), the research division of Hispanic Business Inc., companies spent more than $3.3 billion to market products to Latinos in 2005, a 6.8 percent increase from 2004. According to *Hispanic Business Magazine* (2006) the top companies advertising to the Latino market, Table 1.1, are spending well over $150 million annually to reach the Latino consumer.

In order to tap into this consumer market, however, companies must understand the complexity of the diverse Latino community.

Table 1.1
Top 10 Latino Market Advertisers in 2006

Company	Spending (In Thousands of Dollars)
Lexicon Marketing	162,695
Procter & Gamble	154,278
Univision	99,880
General Motors	91,924
Sears, Roebuck & Company	77,286
Johnson & Johnson	71,677
AT&T	71,244
McDonald's	68,655
Wal-Mart	58,515
PepsiCo	54,921

Source: Media Report. 2006. Top Advertisers in the Hispanic Market. *Hispanic Business,* December.

Organizations are quickly realizing that a single marketing approach does not fit all Latino consumers. Differences are strong enough and affect profits enough that companies are making dedicated efforts to better understand the Latino community.

Organizations first started to establish formalized efforts to reach Latino consumers in the early 1960s. Cuban advertising executives who had come to the United States to get away from Fidel Castro's regime in Cuba convinced U.S. advertisers that there was an untapped Latino consumer market that required unique marketing attention. Initially, advertising and marketing efforts intended to reach Latino consumers simply involved translating current ad campaigns into Spanish. However, often the branding and marketing message was lost in translation when simply converting to Spanish language was the extent of the Latino marketing efforts. Today, companies are much more knowledgeable about the Latino consumer and have recognized that simply advertising in Spanish is an overly unsophisticated view of this market segment. Companies do not define all Anglo consumers across the nation with a one-dimensional segmentation model. Smart marketers have realized that it is not suitable to do so for Latino consumers. According to the Association of Hispanic Advertising Agencies (Kravetz, 2006), the advertising and marketing campaigns used today involve more sophisticated and nuanced ways of connecting with Latino consumers.

For example, a recent article in the newspaper *Crain's Chicago Business* highlighted the story of Indianapolis-based ATA Airlines, which was struggling to determine why it was not having success tapping into the Latino market (Klein, 2007). Their ad slogan was "Use our airline to get away." What the airline company did not realize was that most Latinos do not want to "get away," but instead prefer to spend their vacations with their extended families. The article quoted George San Jose, president of the San Jose Group of Chicago, a leading Latino marketing firm. With this additional insight of Latino culture, the airline changed its slogan to, "The official airline of family vacations." This change resulted in improved acquisition of Latino consumers by ATA.

Other unique aspects of the Latino culture and demographics are providing greater opportunities to some organizations than others. For example, because Latinos have a high birth rate, they tend to have large families. For organizations that sell baby and family products, the Latino market has a huge revenue potential. Other aspects of the Latino community create unique marketing implications for advertisers. For example, as you will learn in Chapter 3, Latinos favor group decision making, tend to avoid conflict, and rely heavily on experts for guidance. Advertisers need to understand such cultural elements and leverage these concepts in their marketing campaigns to better tap into the mindset of the Latino consumer. Aspects of Latino culture can impact other business functions as well. For instance, Latinos tend to have different attitudes toward the concept of time. The implication of this is that companies may want to provide customer service in a different way and during extended time windows to better meet the needs of Latino consumers.

LINK BETWEEN THE WORKPLACE AND MARKETPLACE

Organizations are recognizing that simply partnering with organizations that specialize in Latino marketing is not enough, however. They need to employ increasing numbers of their own Latino employees who can provide additional insight into the mindset of the Latino consumer. These organizations want employees to help them not just with advertising campaigns, but to assist in the development of products and services that are attuned to the characteristics of Latino culture. One organization that has benefited from this approach is PepsiCo, the convenience food and beverage company based in Purchase, New York. Adelante, the Latino employee network at PepsiCo, helped in the development of guacamole-flavored Doritos Tortilla Chips. Members of Adelante provided feedback on the taste and packaging of the product to help ensure it would be regarded as authentic in the Latino community. Their insights helped to make this product one of the most successful new-product launches in PepsiCo's history, generating more than $100 million in sales in its first year alone (Rodriguez, 2006c).

Latino employees in key positions can also help companies better understand the impact of regional clustering of different subgroups within the Latino community. Such insights can help an organization capitalize on cultural nuances by fine-tuning product, distribution, and/or ad messaging according to the *Hispanic/Latino Market Profile* published by the Magazine Publishers of America (2004, p. 8). For example, a company such as McDonald's could introduce a sandwich product in Florida that caters to the Cuban palate and a totally different sandwich product in Los Angeles that appeals to Mexican taste preferences.

Because of the tremendous opportunities that exist within the Latino consumer market, companies are seeking guidance from their Latino employees in a variety of other areas. Organizations also depend on their Latino employees to provide further clarity as to language preferences based on generational patterns and level of acculturation/assimilation. Similarly, companies have realized that since the Latino population is relatively young, many Latinos have not had a chance to establish strong brand loyalty to particular products. With the help of Latino employees, companies can better craft brand messages that appeal to this young Latino market.

Because they know the differences and the similarities within the demographic group, talented Latinos can bring increased business opportunity to their employers. For example, the Hispanic business unit at Merrill Lynch, the wealth management, capital markets, and financial advisory company, generated over $1 billion worth of new business nationwide in 2004, double its goal. Because of the growth of the Latino market, the company decided to hire 100 bilingual Latinos to make further inroads into this Latino consumer market (Grow et al., 2004).

These Latino professionals can contribute marketing insights because they relate well with the Latino ethnic consumer. This is the value of having a workforce that mirrors a company's desired customer profile. For example, only a Latino employee can accurately describe the tension that Latinos face as they try to acculturate into American society and how this impacts the psyche of the Latino consumer. They might recommend marketing campaigns that reference their country of origin, the importance of staying connected to family back home, or images that reinforce a sense of nostalgia (Synovate, 2004). For any company to market its products and services to Latinos effectively, it needs to have individuals in key roles who possess firsthand experience of the culture.

American businesses compete in a vibrant marketplace where customer needs are constantly changing. Meeting those needs effectively requires an ability to adjust quickly. The capability to adjust and adapt quickly to Latino consumer needs lies in the ability for companies to harness the Latino diversity they have within their organization. A failure to tap into a pool of Latino employees will result in an organization's inability to realize the potential that exists within the Latino consumer market. This requires more then simply having Latino employees on staff, however. In order to see diverse prospects, a company must have the ability to learn from their Latino employees and to grow that capability within the organization.

SUMMARY

Human resource and diversity practitioners must begin using the language of business when trying to promote their Latino talent management initiatives. First, human resource and diversity executives can incorporate Latino initiatives as a potential source of intellectual capital to help combat the pending labor shortage due to retiring baby boomers. Doing so will allow a company to remain competitive in the knowledge economy. Second, those in human resource and diversity functions can demonstrate that they understand and appreciate the difficulty of generating new sources of revenue and the pressure of winning new customers. By aligning Latino initiatives as a mechanism to more effectively tap into a growing consumer segment that will soon reach $1 trillion in size, human resource and diversity executives can validate their role in helping to increase sales growth. Improving competitiveness in a knowledge economy and identifying new ways to grow revenue provide human resource and diversity practitioners with a strong business case for Latino talent management initiatives.

CHAPTER 2

LATINO DEMOGRAPHICS AND TERMINOLOGY

Along with understanding the business case for attracting and retaining top Latino talent, organizations must become familiar with key demographic statistics and terms relating to the U.S. Latino population. Improving the level of understanding of the diverse Latino population and chronicling Latinos' growing impact on the nation better prepares organizations and practitioners to develop more inclusive workplace strategies. Organizations such as the Pew Hispanic Center, a nonpartisan research organization in Washington, DC, and the U.S. Census Bureau play an important role in helping organizations improve their understanding of the U.S. Latino population.

A plethora of research reports and statistics have appeared as the result of the rapidly increasing Latino population in the United States. While this is beneficial, it does make it increasingly difficult to identify which data are the most significant. Data exist on topics such as Latino marital status, home ownership levels, household income, and poverty levels. Human resource professionals, diversity practitioners, and business managers looking to better understand the role Latinos are playing in society and in the American workplace should become familiar with the 15 demographic statistics discussed in this chapter. Before addressing the demographic statistics, we'll define some of the key terms associated with the Latino community.

LATINO TERMS

Within the U.S. Latino community, six subgroups have emerged as the main categories for segmentation—Cubans, Mexicans, Puerto Ricans, Spaniards, Central Americans, and South Americans. People who refer to themselves as Hispanic or Latino usually have ancestry from one of the 22 Spanish-speaking countries in Central and South America, the Caribbean, and Europe (Table 2.1). Latinos living in the United States share experiences, principles, and viewpoints that tend to unite them. However, it's important to look not only at how Latinos are similar to one another, but also at how they are different from non-Latinos.

Latinos are a highly diverse group. Because of this, Latinos tend to have different points of view on key topics. One area of contention is the use of the terms Hispanic and Latino. There is a great deal of history and strong feelings regarding these terms within the community. To fully comprehend this difference of opinion, it is best to look deeper into both terms.

Table 2.1
Spanish–Speaking Countries

Argentina	Guatemala
Belize	Honduras
Bolivia	Mexico
Brazil	Nicaragua
Chile	Panama
Colombia	Paraguay
Costa Rica	Peru
Cuba	Puerto Rico
Dominican Republic	Spain
Ecuador	Uruguay
El Salvador	Venezuela

Hispanic

Hispania was the name given by the ancient Romans in 200 B.C. to the whole Iberian Peninsula located in Western Europe. After the fall of the Roman Empire, the Moors, who were North African Muslims, invaded Hispania and eventually divided the Iberian Peninsula into two separate countries, one of which later became known as Spain. Because this area had been called Hispania, it eventually became common to refer to people who could trace their lineage or cultural heritage back to Spain as *Hispanos*.

In 1960, the U.S. Census Bureau was seeking a term to refer to people of Spanish ancestry who were residing in the United States. The U.S. Census Bureau had previously used the term Mexican but this did not differentiate those who were of Latin American descent. Because the Spanish had colonized parts of Latin America and because people in other parts of the world who could trace their lineage to Spain were called Hispanos, the U.S. Census Bureau decided to use the term *Hispanic* to refer to U.S. residents of Spanish ancestry. Eventually, the U.S. Census Bureau expanded the use of the term Hispanic to include those whose origin was Cuba, Central America, Mexico, Puerto Rico, the Spanish Caribbean, and South America.

The term *Hispanic* refers to residents within the United States regardless of whether they are U.S. citizens, permanent residents, or temporary immigrants. Organizations, however, often make the mistake of referring to individuals or programs outside of the United States as Hispanic. For example, some organizations mistakenly refer to someone who is born and raised in Mexico and working at a facility in Mexico as being Hispanic. This is not correct because the individual does not *reside* in the United States. Similarly, some organizations mistakenly refer to efforts to build business and revenue in Latin America as Hispanic initiatives. Such efforts can only be called Hispanic initiatives if the focus is on domestic efforts in the United States.

The term Hispanic appears in the names of several prominent organizations (such as the Hispanic Chamber of Commerce and the National Society of Hispanic MBAs). However, organizations should be careful to use the term correctly. There is a growing trend against using the term Hispanic for a couple of reasons. First, some people resent the fact that Hispanic is an English word that was created by English speakers. These individuals consider the term offensive because it is a word English speakers made up for them. Others have difficulty with the term Hispanic because it invokes thoughts of the Spanish conquest of Latin America and Spanish colonialism. Finally, some people object because Hispanic is gender neutral and does not differentiate between males or females.

Latino

The term *Latino* is an actual Spanish word that refers to people with Latin American ancestry, which includes the Spanish Caribbean, Central and South America, as well as those from Spain. The term first became popular in the 1980s when people in the United States began using Latino as an alternative to the term Hispanic as a way to identify themselves. Although the term has gender connotations—a male is a Latino and a female is a Latina—it follows the usual conventions for Spanish words in that the masculine plural form *Latinos* refers to both males and females collectively. As ethnic pride has grown, so too has the popularity of the term Latino. Many people prefer Latino because it is more closely associated to the people and culture of Latin America as opposed to Spain. Others prefer it because it is a term that has come from within the community as opposed to one made up by those who are not part of the community.

Today, the terms Hispanic and Latino are often used interchangeably by organizations and by many people within the community. However, organizations, managers, human resource professionals, and diversity practitioners need to be aware that the debate over which term to use is more than a battle over names. As D. H. Figueredo (2002) references in his book, *Latino History and Culture,* the conflict involves a power struggle and the attempt by those who have been marginalized in the past to name themselves as opposed to allowing others decide what labels they will use to refer to them (p. 47). For this reason, you run less of a risk of offending someone in this community if you use the term Latino as opposed to the term Hispanic. Also, because the term Latino is more en vogue these days, programs targeting this community that are labeled with the term Hispanic might appear somewhat out of date. Thus, it is recommended that organizations starting new programs and initiatives aimed at this group of people use the term Latino rather than Hispanic.

In addition to the terms Hispanic and Latino, there are many other terms that should be learned by those interacting with members of this community. Many of these terms are associated with race and ethnicity. However, because there is a significant percentage of people within this community who were born outside of the United States, it is generally a good idea to understand common terms associated with immigration status as well. Understanding these terms and using them properly will demonstrate an awareness of Latino diversity that will not be lost on those within the community. Those who understand these terms and use them properly have an advantage over those who lack this knowledge or who use these terms incorrectly. For example, you can imagine the disappointment a Puerto Rican feels when someone mistakenly refers to him as a Chicano as opposed to a Boricua. If you are not aware of these terms related to national origin or immigration status, the following definitions will prove very helpful:

Alien: A term used by the U.S. immigration office to refer to any person who is not a citizen or resident of the United States.

Anglo: The term often used broadly by Latinos to refer to white, non–Latino Americans. It is preferable to white because it highlights the ethno–cultural, rather than the racial basis for distinction (Ferdman and Cortes, 1992).

Boricua: Comes from the word *Boriquén* that was the original name of the island of Puerto Rico before the arrival of the Spanish. The word has come to identify any resident or descendent of Puerto Rico and conveys a strong sense of pride. It is common for Puerto Ricans living in the United States as well as those in Puerto Rico to refer to themselves as either Puerto Rican or Boricua. Some Puerto Ricans believe that only those who were born in Puerto Rico can use the term Boricua and those of Puerto Rican descent but who were born elsewhere cannot.

Caribeño: Refers to an individual whose original country of origin is located in the Spanish-speaking Caribbean.

Chicano: Refers to American citizens of Mexican descent who possess a strong sense of Mexican-American ethnic identity. The term was most widely used in the mid-1960s by Mexican American activists in the Southwest who wanted to convey a unique ethnic identity. In the 1970s, Chicano was actually the preferred, politically correct term to use in reference to Mexican Americans and was widely used in the field of sociology. Eventually, the term became quite politicized and eventually fell out of preference as the appropriate term to refer to the entire population. Latinos not of Mexican descent do not tend to use the term to refer to themselves.

Cubano: A person born in Cuba or born in the United States but having Cuban ancestry.

Documented immigrant: Includes both legal and illegal immigrants residing in the United States who have been counted by the U.S. Census; an individual whose name and address appears on some type of legal or official document.

Green card: Officially known as a Permanent Resident Card, this document provides evidence of lawful permanent resident status in the United States. The card also allows foreign nationals to live, work legally, travel abroad, and return to the United States. Green card holders may also apply for U.S. citizenship after a certain period of time.

Illegal immigrant: People who cross national borders in a way that violates the immigration laws of the destination country.

Mestizo: Persons of mixed Spanish or Portuguese heritage and American Indian indigenous ancestry.

Mexican: Someone born and raised in Mexico. An American citizen of Mexican descent and heritage who prefers to be identified with his or her dominant Latino heritage. Individuals need not be born in Mexico to refer to themselves as Mexican.

Mexican American: American citizen of full or partial Mexican origin or descent. The term is most commonly used in Texas and other parts of the Southwest. A Mexican American does not necessarily need to be of Anglo ancestry.

Mulato: Person of mixed Spanish or Portuguese heritage and African ancestry.

Naturalized citizen: An individual who has become a U.S. citizen after successfully immigrating to the United States following proper immigration procedures. Naturalized citizens receive an official document issued by the Department of Homeland Security.

Non-Hispanic: Refers to all persons who do not claim Hispanic or Latino ethnicity. Since Latinos can be white, black, or brown skinned, it is common to use the term non-Hispanic white to refer to an Anglo.

Nuyorican: A Puerto Rican from New York who equally embraces their New York and Puerto Rican identity. Sometimes also spelled New Yorican.

Permanent resident: Any person who is not a citizen of the United States and who lives in the United States lawfully and legally.

Quisqueyano: Someone of Dominican Republic descent. Quisqueya was the original island name of the Dominican Republic before the arrival of the Spanish.

Raza: A Spanish term that literally means race but is most often used to mean the people. Generally refers to the people of Mexican and indigenous ancestry. The phrase *Viva la Raza* means "long live the people/race" and is often linked with the Chicano movement. According to The National Council of La Raza, a national Latino civil rights and advocacy organization, the term was coined by Mexican scholar José Vasconcelos and reflects the fact that people of Latin America are a mixture of the world's races, cultures, and religions. The term is not generally embraced by Latinos who are not of Mexican ancestry.

Tejano: A Mexican American born and raised in Texas.

These terms are powerful because they help Latinos define themselves in their own minds and in the eyes of others. Understanding these terms and using them properly allows for better communication with Latinos in the workplace and avoids generic approaches that often prove to be ineffective (Chong and Baez, 2005).

KEY LATINO STATISTICS: THE L15

Along with being familiar with and understanding Latino terminology, it is also important for those involved in Latino initiatives or who are working with Latinos to gain a better appreciation of the size, scope, and unique aspects attributed to this community. While there are numerous numerical and statistical elements (demographics) about this community that can be explored, there are 15 items that organizations, managers, human resource executives, and diversity practitioners should know. Throughout the rest of this book, these metrics and statistics will be referred to as the Latino 15 or simply as L15.

L1: Population

In the late 1960s, the U.S. population reached 200 million. At that time, the Latino population accounted for 4.2 percent of the population or 8.5 million people. In 2006, the U.S. population reached 300 million. Of this 300 million, current estimates by the Pew Hispanic Center put the Latino population at 44.7 million or roughly 15 percent of the total U.S. population. This means that since the 1960s, the Latino population is now 5 times as large and its representation in the total population has almost quadrupled. According to the Pew Hispanic Center (2006a), Latinos accounted for 36 percent of the 100 million people added to the population in the past four decades, more than any other ethnic group. To help put this population figure in perspective, consider the fact that there are more Latinos living in the United States than there are Canadians in Canada (population of about 33 million) or Spaniards in Spain (population of about 44 million).

The size of the Latino population becomes even more impressive when you consider that Latinos are also the fastest-growing demographic in the United States. According to projections by Ramírez and de la Cruz (2002), between 2000 and 2020 the Latino labor force will grow by an astounding 77 percent, while the non-Latino labor force will grow by only 9 percent. Projections by the

U.S. Census Bureau indicate that Latinos will represent close to 25 percent of the U.S. population by the year 2050.

According to estimates by the Pew Hispanic Center (Passel, 2006) of the 44.7 million Latinos in the United States, approximately 12 million are unauthorized migrant Latinos. This means that roughly 26 percent of the Latino population in the United States are not U.S. citizens or have not been granted permanent resident status. Of the approximately 12 million unauthorized Latino migrants, about 7.2 million were employed, accounting for 4.9 percent of the civilian labor force. The size of the Latino population and its continued rapid growth are key reasons why organizations are looking to better understand this significant demographic group.

L2: Place of Origin

According to the U.S. Census Bureau (2000), 63 percent of the Latinos in the United States claim Mexico as their place of origin. Puerto Ricans are the next largest subgroup within the Latino community at approximately 10 percent. Cubans make up 4 percent of the U.S. Latino community. People who claim El Salvador and the Dominican Republic as their place of origin come in at 3 percent each of the total U.S. Latino population. Individuals from the remaining South American countries make up 5 percent of the population and those from the other Central American countries represent 4 percent of the population.

For organizations and practitioners, it is important to have a good understanding of the diversity that exists within the U.S. Latino population. Knowing that Latinos of Mexican descent make up almost two thirds of the U.S. Latino community could impact staffing and marketing decisions related to this community. Companies looking to maximize their ability to connect with the Latino community might be well served by identifying with Mexican cultural characteristics.

L3: Average Age

The U.S. Latino community is quite young. According to a study conducted by the Pew Hispanic Center (2006b), the average age of U.S. Latinos is 27 years. Conversely, the average age of Anglos in the United States is 40 years of age. Latinos thus have a higher proportion of young adults and children and fewer elderly than the rest of the non-Latino population. Approximately 56.1 percent of Latinos are under the age of 30 compared to only 37 percent of Anglos being under the age of 30. Similarly, 41.4 percent of Anglos are over the age of 45 while only 20 percent of Latinos are over 45. The relatively young Latino population is magnified when you consider that the Anglo population and the African American population are not only stable in size but also aging.

The young age for Latinos means that many have simply not gained much work experience and may partly explain why there are fewer Latinos in senior management positions. This also means that Latinos in the workplace may be in positions that would benefit greatly from an increased focus on management and leadership development programs.

L4: Place of Birth

According to the Pew Hispanic Center (2006b), of the total U.S. Latino population, 59.8 percent were born in the United States. The remaining 40.2 percent were born outside of the United States. This is an important statistic for organizations to know because of language proficiency, immigration status, and education levels.

L5: Place of Residence

Figures from the U.S. Census Bureau (2005) indicate that close to half (48.7 percent) of all Latinos in the United States reside in just two states, California and Texas. States with the highest percentage of Latino population are:

State	Percentage
New Mexico	42
California	32.4
Texas	32
Arizona	25
Nevada	19
Colorado	17.1
Florida	16.8
New York	15.1
New Jersey	13.3
Illinois	12.3

Figure 2.1 shows a graphic representation of the Latino population by state.

Figure 2.1
Latino Population by State

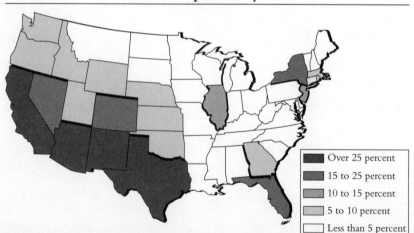

Over 25 percent
15 to 25 percent
10 to 15 percent
5 to 10 percent
Less than 5 percent

Note: Alaska and Hawaii have less then 5 percent Latino papulation each.
Source: U.S. Census Bureau 2005.

The population breakdown is important for two reasons. First, if companies are looking to recruit Latino professionals, they need to target those states with high Latino populations. If an organization is in a state with a low Latino population, they may want to attend Latino career fairs and recruiting events in nearby states with higher Latino populations to attract Latino talent. Second, companies can look at their consumer population and see if their customers reside in states with a high Latino population. If so, it should raise its sense of the urgency of Latino initiatives because there are consumer segment implications.

L6: Birth Rates

Latino immigrants, most of them young adults in their prime child-bearing years, have birth rates twice as high as those of non-Latinos. When compared to Anglos, Latinos have a much higher percentage of their population in child-bearing years. In fact, the birth rate for Latinos is 3.3 children, almost twice that of Anglos (1.9 children). Consequently, Latino population growth in the next few decades will be driven primarily by increases in second-generation Latinos. This means that Latino population growth will be driven by the birth of Latinos as opposed to Latino immigration into the United States.

In comparison, the Anglo population is remaining relatively flat due to their higher average age and lower birth rate. The birth-to-death rate of each group shows the striking differences in the birth rates of these two groups. According to the National Center for Health Statistics, for each Anglo child that is born, one Anglo dies resulting in a 1 to 1 birth-to-death ratio. The birth-to-death ratio in the Latino community is 8 to 1 meaning that eight Latino children are born for each Latino who dies. Such birth-to-death ratios make it easy to see why the Latino community is growing so rapidly.

L7: Generation

There are at least four generations of Latinos in the United States. First-generation Latinos are those who were born outside of the country but now reside in the United States. Second-generation Latinos are born in the United States with at least one parent born outside of the country. Third-generation Latinos are the U.S. born children of U.S. born Latino parents (Suro and Passel, 2003). First-generation immigrants tend to adhere to their cultural values and language as they make adjustments and experience the acculturation process. If they came to the United States as adults, cultural values are modified out of necessity as they adjust. Many modify their behavior at work to adapt to the new culture, while at home they act as if they were still in their home country (Domino and Acosta, 1987; Gallegos and Ferdman, 2007). Table 2.2 highlights the number of Latinos in each generation group from 1980 to 2020.

L8: Language Preferences

Within the Latino community, about 47 percent of the people predominantly speak Spanish, 28 percent are bilingual, and 25 percent are English dominant (Suro et al., 2002). Most first-generation Latinos speak Spanish, second-generation Latinos tend to be

Table 2.2
Latino Population, Actual and Projected 1980–2020 (in millions)

Year	First Generation	Second Generation	Third-Plus Generation
1980	5.1	4.0	5.5
1990	9.1	6.1	7.1
2000	14.2	9.9	11.3
2010	18.1	15.4	14.2
2020	20.6	21.7	18.2

Source: U.S. Census Bureau for 1980 to 2000; Pew Hispanic Center and Urban Institute for projections for 2010 and 2020.

bilingual, and those of the third and fourth generations are likely to be English speakers as highlighted in Table 2.3.

Of Latinos who are born in the United States, 61 percent are English dominant, 35 percent are bilingual, and only 4 percent are Spanish dominant. The language preference is quite different for those Latinos born outside of the United States with 72 percent indicating they are Spanish dominant, 24 percent being bilingual, and only 4 percent English dominant. Human resource professionals, diversity practitioners, managers, and marketing executives should notice such language preferences because they have huge implications on recruiting and consumer advertising.

L9: Educational Attainment

If you compare the percentage of the population of the major racial and ethnic groups in the United States, Latinos rank at the bottom when it comes to educational attainment. According to the Pew Hispanic Center (2006b), only about 12 percent of the current U.S. Latino population has earned a bachelor's degree. This is less than half of the Anglo population where 30 percent of the population has a bachelor's degree. In comparison, 17 percent of the African Americans have earned a bachelor's degree and Asian Americans have

Table 2.3
Latino Language Preference by Generation

Language	First Generation (%)	Second Generation (%)	Third-Plus Generation (%)
English Dominant	4	46	78
Bilingual	24	47	22
Spanish Dominant	72	7	–

Data from Roberto Suro, Mollyann Brodie, Annie Steffenson, Jaime Valdes, and Rebecca Levin. 2002. *2002 National Survey of Latinos*. Washington, DC: Pew Hispanic Center.

the highest percentage of educational attainment with over 49 percent having earned a bachelor's degree. Since there are approximately 44.7 million Latinos in the United States, if 12 percent have a bachelor's degree, this equates to approximately 5.3 million Latinos.

According to U.S. Census (2006b) data, there are approximately 557,000 Latinos in the United States who have earned a master's degree. This means that of those who do earn a bachelor's degree, only about 10 percent go on to obtain a master's degree. The U.S. Census data also indicates that there are approximately 95,000 Latinos in the United States who hold doctorate degrees. However, given that there are 44.7 million Latinos in the United States, this represents less than 1 percent of the total U.S. Latino population. Attainment of a college education is not possible without first finishing high school. Among U.S. Latinos, only 58 percent finish high school versus a 90 percent high school completion rate for Anglos. The level of Latino educational attainment as a percent of the population also varies by place of origin as highlighted in Table 2.4. Latinos of Mexican descent have the lowest level of educational attainment and those of Cuban descent have the highest.

Further exploring these statistics provides some interesting insights. Of Latinos who are born in the United States, 73 percent go on to finish high school, 40 percent obtain some college education,

Table 2.4
Educational Attainment by Origin (Percent of Population)

	High School Diploma	Undergraduate Degree
Mexican	51.9	7.9
Puerto Rican	71.8	14.0
Cuban	72.1	24.0
Average of all U.S. Latinos	58.4	12.1
Anglo Average	90.0	30.6

Data from U.S. Census Bureau. 2006b. *Current Population Survey: 2005 Annual Social and Economic Supplement,* October 26.

and 14 percent earn a bachelor's degree (Pew Hispanic Center, 2006b). What brings these figures down is the 40 percent of the Latino population that is born outside of the United States who tend to have much lower levels of educational attainment. Latino students now make up the largest minority group in the school-age population in the country. Yet they lag behind their white Anglo and Asian peers—and in some cases African Americans—on most measures of achievement: test scores, college completion, dropout rates.

L10: Industries

Over 51 percent of Latinos in the United States work in jobs in the service, construction, and production industries (U.S. Census Bureau, 2006b). The high representation of Latinos who work in these industries is reflective of their lower level of education and limited proficiency of English. As Table 2.5 indicates, only 16.8 percent of Latinos are in management or professional occupations compared to 39.1 percent of the Anglo population holding such positions.

Table 2.5
Occupation by Origin (Percent of Population)

	Production and Transportation	Construction and Maintenance	Service and Administrative	Management and Professional
Mexican	21.1	17.6	24.4	14.0
Puerto Rican	15.6	9.7	22.4	23.8
Cuban	15.3	10.1	16.9	29.3
Average of all U.S. Latinos	19.5	15.5	24.6	16.8
Anglo Average	11.3	9.1	13.4	39.1

Data from U.S. Census Bureau. 2006b. *Current Population Survey: 2005 Annual Social and Economic Supplement,* October 26.

As shown in Table 2.5, Latinos of Mexican descent are the least likely to hold managerial and professional positions. Because of the sizeable proportions of managerial and professional workers among the Cuban immigrants who came to the United States in the 1960s, it is no surprise that they have one of the highest proportions employed in these occupations among U.S. Latinos.

L11: Annual Earnings

Education is the single biggest reason for the gaps in earnings and employment between Latinos and Anglos (Badillo, 2006; Reimers, 1992). Only 13.8 percent of all Latinos earn more than $50,000 per year annually versus the 35 percent of Anglos who earn more than $50,000 per year. This means that Anglos are 2.5 times more likely to earn $50,000 or more per year than Latinos as highlighted in Table 2.6.

L12: Entrepreneurship

The U.S. Economic Census conducted by the U.S. Census Bureau (2006a) indicates there are over 2 million Latino business owners in the United States generating $300 billion in annual sales. The number of Latino-owned businesses in the United States is

Table 2.6
Yearly Earnings by Origin (Percent of Population)

	$35K to $50K	*$50K to $75K*	*$75K Plus*
Mexican	15.2	8.3	2.8
Puerto Rican	19.3	13.0	5.4
Cuban	16.4	14.1	11.0
Average of all U.S. Latinos	15.6	9.4	4.4
Anglo Average	22.5	19.4	15.6

Data from U.S. Census Bureau. 2006b. *Current Population Survey: 2005 Annual Social and Economic Supplement,* October 26.

expected to grow 55 percent in the next six years up to 3.2 million with total revenue surging to more than $465 billion according to estimates by HispanTelligence. This makes Latino entrepreneurs the fastest growing entrepreneur segment in the United States as stated by the U.S. Small Business Administration (2007). Latinos in the United States are opening businesses at a rate that is three times as fast as the national average according to reports by the U.S. Census Bureau (2006a).

Four states, California, Texas, Florida, and New York account for over 70 percent of the firms owned by Latinos according to the U.S. Census Bureau (2006a). Interestingly, Latinas represent the fastest growing entrepreneurial sector in the U.S. business community according to the Center for Women's Research (2000). Latinas are becoming entrepreneurs at six times the rate of the national average and women now own a third of all Hispanic firms.

L13: Politics

Latinos are predominantly Democrats. According to the William C. Velazquez Institute and the Pew Hispanic Center (2006c), the 2006 national exit poll showed that in elections for the U.S. House of Representatives, 69 percent of Latinos voted for Democrats and only 30 percent voted for Republicans. This tendency has huge implications regarding the future political landscape in the United States.

There are currently over 5,000 Latino officials serving in all levels of government according to the U.S. Hispanic Leadership Institute (2006). While this may sound like an impressive number, it is only a fraction of the total number of elected positions in the U.S. government. Even though Latinos comprise about 15 percent of the population, they account for only 1 percent of all elected officials. If the Latino population expects to have their perspectives and opinions acted on by the government, tremendous strides must be made to increase the representation of Latinos elected to government office.

L14: Religious Preferences

According to a national survey conducted by the Hispanic Churches in American Public Life (Espinosa, Elizondo, and Miranda, 2003), 70 percent of Latinos are Catholic, 23 percent are Protestant or "other Christian" (includes Jehovah's Witnesses and Mormons), and only about 1 percent of Latinos identify with Buddhism, Islam, or Judaism. Since Latinos tend to place a high emphasis on their spirituality, observance of religious events and holidays is very important.

L15: Purchasing Power

As was already highlighted in Chapter 1, the U.S. Latino consumer market is estimated at $800 billion, making it one of the 10 largest economies in the world. Expected to reach $1 trillion by 2010.

SUMMARY

This chapter provided a foundation of knowledge about the Latino community that most people do not possess, including many Latinos. The chapter included both qualitative information and quantitative data that provides a better holistic perspective of the Latino community. Organizational leaders should leverage the terminology shared in this chapter to improve their ability to communicate with and about Latinos. The Latino15, a summary of which is provided in Table 2.7, allows for a deeper level of analysis of the size and scope of the U.S. Latino community.

Additionally, the L15 provides metrics that organizations can track and analyze to help identify trends and opportunities within the Latino community. The insights highlighted in this chapter provide organizations with an advanced and informed perspective with which to establish Latino talent management initiatives.

Table 2.7
The Latino 15 (L15)

L1	Population size	44.7 million—15% of U.S. population
L2	Place of origin	63% Mexico, 10% Puerto Rico, 4% Cuba
L3	Average age	Latinos 27; Anglos 40
L4	Place of birth	59.8% born in U.S.; 40.2% born outside United States
L5	Place of residence	48.7% of all U.S. Latinos live in California or Texas
L6	Birth rate	Latinos average 3.3 children; Anglos average 1.9 children
L7	Generation	14.2 million (first generation); 9.9 million (second generation); 11.3 million (third generation +) in 2000
L8	Language	47% Spanish dominant; 28% bilingual; 25% English dominant
L9	Education	58.4% have HS diploma; 12.1% have a bachelor's degree
L10	Industries	16.8% of Latino population in management or professional jobs
L11	Annual earnings	13% of Latinos earn over $50K per year; 35% of Anglos earn over $50K annually
L12	Entrepreneurship	Latinos becoming entrepreneurs at 3 times the rate of Anglos
L13	Politics	69% vote Democrat and hold about 1% of elected office positions
L14	Religion	70% Catholic; 23% Protestant or "other Christian"
L15	Market size	Estimated at $800 billion in 2007; expected to reach $1 trillion by 2010

CHAPTER 3

LATINO CULTURAL ASPECTS

When differences associated with ethnic diversity are not distinguished and valued, people tend to engage in stereotyping, prejudice, and discrimination (Carr-Ruffino, 2003). Such has been the experience of many Latinos in the workplace. Over 54 percent of Latinos indicate that they have seen an increase in discrimination against them (Suro and Escobar, 2006). These Latinos felt that in the past five years, they have experienced discrimination including not being hired or promoted for a job and being called names or insulted. A similar study (Pew Hispanic Center and Kaiser Family Foundation, 2004) indicated that the vast majority of Latinos surveyed feel that discrimination against Latinos is a problem in schools (75 percent) and in the workplace (78 percent).

Along with discrimination, Latinos are also the victim of common negative stereotypes including being perceived as being too passive and lacking the conviction necessary to be a good manager or being too emotional to fill leadership positions (Carr-Ruffino, 2003). These stereotypes often are the result of a lack of understanding about how cultural principles and traditions common in the Latino community impact actions and behaviors. This is why it is so critical for leaders to broaden and deepen their understanding of Latino cultural characteristics. Doing so will not only help to create a more inclusive workplace, it will also enhance productivity and increase the probability of employee success.

To gain appreciation for the richness of the Latino heritage requires an exploration and understanding of the Latino *cultural script*. A cultural script is a pattern of social interaction and communication that is characteristic of a particular cultural group (Triandis et al., 1984). Having a strong cultural script and a common linkage to Latin American ancestry have been cited as the main features that distinguish Latinos as a group (Marger, 1991). The cultural script of a Latino leads to behaviors that are natural and appropriate to them, but these behaviors and tendencies could be misunderstood or misinterpreted by non-Latinos (Ferdman and Cortes, 1992).

Before looking at specific programs organizations use to recruit, retain, and develop Latino professionals, it is important to have a stronger comprehension of the Latino worldview: How do Latinos see reality based on their heritage? There are many unique elements to the Latino culture and companies wanting to enhance the effectiveness of their talent management strategies should take steps to better understand these aspects.

The sharing of aspects common within the Latino community is not intended to promote further stereotypes or make overly broad assumptions. The aim in sharing these aspects of Latino culture is to highlight common patterns and values held by Latinos with the understanding that they will be expressed at various strengths depending on age, level of acculturation, and the individual's sense of Latino identity.

Those involved in crafting talent management strategies should look at the various elements described in this chapter to see how they may impact the effectiveness of such initiatives. Having a better sense of appreciation for how Latinos tend to view the world around them provides insight into why new approaches should be used when crafting future talent management practices related to the Latino employee population. In essence, this chapter highlights

Table 3.1
The Latino Cultural Script

Interaction Tendencies	Spirituality and Family	Sense of Identity
Collectivism	Familism	Ethnic identity
Simpatía	Machismo	Cultural identity
Respeto	Religion	Acculturation
Personalismo	Time	Assimilation
Communication		

both those things that unite Latinos, as well as what makes Latinos different from non-Latinos. In particular, this chapter explores the three areas of the Latino cultural script, including Latino interaction tendencies, their views on spirituality and family, and their sense of identity (Table 3.1). While not all of these elements are present in each and every Latino, it is the combination of these elements that helps to define a Latino.

INTERACTION TENDENCIES

Interaction tendencies refer to the ways in which Latinos relate to each other and toward those who are not Latino. This is an aspect of the Latino cultural script that is unique to Latinos. The areas that impact how Latinos tend to interact with others include collectivism, *respeto, simpatía, personalismo,* and communication. These interaction tendencies shape how Latinos build relationships, whose needs they put first, and their communication style.

Collectivism

Latinos tend to have a high sense of collectivism, which is one of the five cultural value dimensions defined by social psychologist Geert Hofstede (1980). The tendency to display collectivist behaviors means that Latinos will tend to place the needs and goals of the group before the needs and goals of an individual. Therefore, Latinos often work to promote unity, harmony, and success at the group level. The collectivist style of most Latinos means that life revolves around group or community interests and having a sense of belonging to a group receives high priority. The collectivist mindset of Latinos also drives behaviors that promote cooperation and collaboration with others. Other characteristics of collectivist cultures include a high sense of importance on achieving group goals, a desire to have equal distribution of rewards within a group, and a strong sense of loyalty to a group (Salgado de Snyder and Nelly, 1987). The collectivist mindset allows Latinos to have a "we" mentality and being a part of a group often results in a strong sense of belonging (Kikoski and Kikoski, 1999).

The Latino emphasis on identification with and loyalty to a group can have implications in the workplace because it is quite common for an organization to stress achievement and accomplishment on an individual level (Marín and Marín, 1991). For example, for some Latinos, loyalty to a group and a friend may be more important than getting a promotion and some Latinos may have a hard time imagining themselves supervising their peers (Chong and Baez, 2005, p. 135). The collectivist approach of Latinos also creates a propensity to use group decision-making models and to promote decisions that are in the best interests of the group.

Some see collectivism as the most important cultural difference between Latinos and non-Latinos (Triandis, 1985). Organizational leaders should take the collectivist outlook into consideration when developing talent management practices so that they can be more inclusive to Latinos. For example, organizations may want to investigate having team goals, as opposed to individual goals, as part of performance appraisals or creating reward systems that recognize a group as opposed to an individual.

Simpatía

Simpatía is a Spanish word that refers to a "general tendency toward avoiding personal conflict, emphasizing positive behaviors in agreeable situations, and de-emphasizing negative behaviors in conflictive circumstances" (Triandis et al., 1984). The Latino culture embraces *simpatía* and promotes a desire to maintain smooth, pleasant social relations with others. Because of this inclination, Latinos are often referred to as being easy to talk to, friendly, and polite.

Simpatía also means that Latinos possess a general orientation to avoid conflict, confrontation, and negative situations (Marín and Marín, 1991). This results in a tendency to suppress disapproval or behaviors that could be considered forceful or overly aggressive. Sometimes, in order to maintain *simpatía,* Latinos will concede to the desires of others in order to convey agreement and to maintain a harmonious relationship. Some Latinos will comply with others even if they disagree because they want others to think well of them (Carr-Ruffino, 2003, p. 347). *Simpatía* also causes some Latinos to appear to be in agreement even if they do not understand a decision or question. To a non-Latino manager, this behavior can be confusing but it should not be construed to indicate that a Latino is passive, lacks conviction, or does not have a defendable point of view. They are simply following their cultural script.

Because of the importance the Latino culture places on harmonious behaviors, a lack of *simpatía* expressed by a coworker, manager, or recruiter toward a Latino could seriously hinder the possibility of establishing a strong relationship. Since *simpatía* impacts how Latinos interact with those around them, it is critical that non-Latinos understand the importance of positive interpersonal relationships in the workplace.

Respeto

Respect (or *respeto,* the Spanish word for respect) values automatic deference to authority. Unlike Anglos, who tend to believe people need to earn their respect, Latinos tend to grant respect more readily to those in positions of power. Since Latin American cultures tend to treat their elderly with a high sense of regard, Latinos readily grant respect to those who are older than they are regardless of their position. Similarly, Latinos also show respect to those they perceive to be experts, including community leaders, teachers, and doctors.

Part of the reason that respect is granted so readily by Latinos is that personal power is derived from being treated with respect. Therefore, a person who is considered to be powerful is automatically granted respect (Marín and Marín, 1991). Those who are considered knowledgeable, powerful, and experienced are deemed to fundamentally possess inner strength, courage, and truthfulness and are thus worthy of respect.

Seeing it as a lack of respect, Latinos tend to avoid criticizing, challenging, or expressing contradictory opinions to their managers. In Latin American cultures, confronting a superior, especially in public, is considered to be disobedient and breaks the bond between an employee and a supervisor (Elvira and Davila, 2005, p. 8). Thus, accepting instructions without question from their managers, even when a task seems unreasonable, is a way that a Latino shows respect (DeForest, 1994). This is a cultural behavior that can lead to stereotypes. Whereas Latinos may see themselves as being respectful, non-Latinos may view Latinos as being passive or subservient (Sosa, 1999).

The Latino dimension of respect thus has implications for an employer. For example, non-Latinos who manage a Latino workgroup should be taught to show appreciation for the respect that has been granted to them. Also, companies should consider having seminars and training sessions led by supervisors or experts, as opposed to peers, to help gain further buy-in of the session objectives. Also, leaders in the Latino community should be leveraged to help with recruiting efforts (see Chapter 4).

Personalismo

This term reflects an expectation by Latinos that their supervisors be warm, friendly, and willing to take an active interest in their personal lives. To a Latino, when a supervisor conveys *personalismo* toward them, it means that the supervisor has an interest in them as a person, and not just an employee. Since Latinos grant respect to their superiors, they expect their superiors to reciprocate by demonstrating *personalismo*. Having superiors show a concern for and involvement with their employees is perceived as a vital aspect of getting work done by those in the Latino community. It is viewed as an approach that can bring with it both professional and personal rewards (Ferdman and Cortes, 1992).

Supervisors can convey *personalismo* by periodically holding one-on-one discussions with their Latino employees and showing a sincere interest in getting to know them as individuals. This, however, may seem uncomfortable to a non-Latino manager who may be more accustomed to maintaining an objective and detached relationship with his or her direct reports. Also, companies should not discourage Latino managers from having strong, personal relationships with their employees due to fears that it may prevent them from being objective.

If *personalismo* is established between employees and their supervisors, it will often lead to a stronger sense of loyalty toward the manager as opposed to the organization as a whole. When a well-respected manager leaves an organization for another employer in close proximity, it is not uncommon to have his Latino employees want to leave with him as a way to maintain continuity.

As a group, Latinos seek a workplace where they can build relationships with people they can trust and who can provide support when needed (d'Iribarne, 2002). By leveraging the aspects of collectivism, *simpatía,* respect, and *personalismo,* Latinos interact with others in effective ways that allow them to build such relationships.

SPIRITUALITY AND FAMILY

Along with their interaction tendencies, Latinos are also unique with the devotion they tend to have toward their spirituality and families. The motive often given as to why Latinos work is their strong sense of duty toward their religion and family (Chong and Baez, 2005, p. 126). The importance placed on spirituality and family also impacts how they form relationships in the workplace and their attitude toward time. Organizational leaders will find knowing more about how Latinos view spirituality and family very helpful in allowing them to understand why Latinos act and behave in the sometimes unique way they do. Ultimately, Latinos tend to view spirituality and family as a resource, as opposed to a barrier to personal achievement.

Familism

Organizations looking to better understand Latinos should try to fully grasp the strong feelings they have toward their family. The pillar of Latino culture is the family that includes not only immediate family members, but the extended family of grandparents, aunts, uncles, and cousins. In the Latino family structure, grandparents and the elderly are honored and revered and are sought out frequently to provide guidance and advice. In Latino societies, the family plays a dominant role and is considered the most important social institution (Marín and Marín, 1991). Family closeness is an important priority and family obligations will often take precedent over individual aspirations (Carr-Ruffino, 2003). Some believe that Latinos place the family at the center of their existence more so than most ethnic groups. The result of this Latino value is an extended family system that is extremely close and unified. Also, the family unit tends to become even stronger during times of crisis.

Because the family is at the center of the Latino culture, the family is always a top priority and there is an intense desire to protect the family. This results in a strong sense of commitment, obligation, and responsibility to help out other family members when they are in need. Many Latinos thus view their jobs as important only because it provides a means for them to support their family. Because Latinos place such a high level of importance on the family unit, Latino employees will often base work decisions and expectations on their family needs (Diaz-Saenz and Witherspoon, 2000). Latinos may also shy away from career aspirations that require them to make family life a lower priority (Chong and Baez, 2005). For example, the strong cultural value to be close to one's family often hinders a Latino's job mobility and career advancement (Bean and Tienda, 1987). If a Latino employee is asked to relocate to another location, it is not uncommon for the entire extended family to be involved in such a decision (Carr-Ruffino, 2003). Similarly, some Latino students are likely to go to a nearby college, even if their grades qualify them for finer universities farther away, simply so that they can remain close to their families (Sosa, 1999).

Because Latinos are more likely to put family concerns first, work life balance is an important issue. This is important for employers to understand because it can play a critical role if substantial work demands or overtime requirements conflict with family obligations. On the other hand, some organizations can leverage this commitment to family to their benefit. For example, granting additional time off with pay so that Latinos can spend more time with family could serve as an attractive incentive-based reward.

The key lesson for organizations is the realization that for Latinos, the family unit is at the center of their existence. Whereas Anglos might seek wealth and power as a way to gain visibility and recognition, Latinos might seek such things as a means to improve their family life (Chong and Baez, 2005, p. 128).

Machismo

In Latino culture, machismo refers to positive male aspects including having courage, honor, and the respect of others. It also conveys the notion that a Latino male can provide for his family and can protect them from harm. Unfortunately, some outside of the Latino culture believe that machismo refers to male dominance. To Latinos, machismo represents efforts to ensure the continuation of family pride and respect. Thus, machismo is closely connected to the strong sense of family held by most Latinos.

In the workplace, machismo can be displayed by either a Latino or a Latina manager and usually manifests itself through an obligation to maintain the health and happiness of their direct reports. It is not uncommon, for example, to have a Latino entrepreneur encourage his employees to think of themselves as a family and to insist that his employees come to him in times of need. In Latin American countries, supervisors feel an even stronger sense of personal obligation to protect their employees (Osland, de Franco, and Osland, 1999). Such strong feelings could be carried over to the American workplace if the Latino is a first-generation immigrant in the country.

Some U.S. employers are concerned that machismo could be taken to an extreme by some Latinos. Such cases could result in a sense of resentment if a male has to report to a female supervisor. However, for the most part, organizations have experienced the positive aspects of machismo in the form of a paternalistic leadership mentality.

Religion

When the Spanish colonized Latin America, they brought with them clergymen who were told to spread Catholicism. Because the church was backed by the Spanish Crown, Spanish priests were given a great deal of power and they quickly established churches, and built cathedrals, hospitals, and even universities. From the 1490s to the 1800s, the Catholic Church essentially oversaw the Spanish colonization of Latin America (Figueredo, 2002, p. 163).

Because of this history and tradition, Latinos tend to have a strong disposition toward religion and spirituality. While Latinos follow many different faiths, Catholicism still remains the religion practiced by the majority of Latinos. The behavior of many Latinos is affected by the strength of their religious beliefs. Latinos with strong religious convictions feel a powerful sense of devotion and worship to God and the Virgin Mary. From an early age, Latinos are taught to express their religious beliefs through various gestures and behaviors such as blessings, candle lighting, holy water, statues, rosary praying, and promises to God (Elvira and Davila, 2005, p. 10). The Latino faith is so pervasive, that it is common to hear Latinos extend such blessings to each other as "*Vaya con Díos*" (go with God) or "*Que Díos te bendiga*" (may God bless you).

The icon of Our Lady of Guadalupe is one of the most identifiable symbols of Latino religion. So strong is the Latino connection to this icon that preparations are already underway for the year 2031 which marks the five hundredth anniversary of the appearance of a "lady from Heaven" to a peasant named Juan Diego in Mexico City in 1531. The lady identified herself as the Virgin Holy Mary, Mother of the True God, Lord of heaven and earth. Latino spirituality is so strong that it is common for Latinos to pray to Our Lady of Guadalupe, God, and other saints to assist with everyday matters related to family and to solve work-related issues.

It is also worth noting that there are some who believe that the priests who helped the Spanish colonize Latin America taught Latinos to be subservient and obedient to those in authority as a way to express their faith in God. It is argued that the teaching of such behaviors in the name of religion made it easier for the Spanish conquerors by creating an oppressed underclass whose collective psyche became rooted in passivity (Sosa, 1999, p. 2). Whether people choose to believe this or deny it is not as important as understanding that Latino religion is deeply rooted in the culture. So much so that some Latinos might feel offended if they are discouraged from talking about religion or demonstrating their faith in the workplace. Similarly, Latinos often place great importance in participating in religious or church events, even if it means missing work. One of the reasons that Latinos revere sacred holidays and religious commitments with such enthusiasm is that they want to remain in the good graces of God. Latinos believe that one's workplace success, health condition, and family happiness are deemed a reflection of God's approval or disapproval of their actions and behaviors (Chong and Baez, 2005, p. 43).

Time

Latinos tend to view time as a precious commodity that should be savored and that their focus should be on being engaged in the here, the now, and the present moment. To a Latino, time is something that needs to be enjoyed and not rushed. Latinos have a tendency to change plans often and easily and can be quite spontaneous, often going on trips with little prior planning or dropping by the house of others unannounced.

Placing an emphasis on making the most out of time, Latinos may also believe that time is relatively relaxed and flexible. They may consider a time commitment as more of a guideline as opposed to a rigid commitment. This view toward time can be quite different from an Anglo's view. To Anglos, time is money and therefore it should not be wasted. Also, Anglos tend to have a more rigid view of time, making sure to start and stop "on time." Anglos also are more future oriented making sure to plan in advance whenever possible.

But an analysis of how Latinos view time needs to encompass a broader perspective than just how they look at a clock or a schedule. It also has to do with how they view their destiny because this is strongly connected to their spirituality. Some Latinos believe that one's destiny and path in life is controlled by God. Those who believe this tend to have a yielding view on life and prepare themselves to consent to God's predetermined fate for them (Alcalay, Sabogal, and Gribble, 1992). That is one reason that Latinos tend to focus on the present moment: because the future is uncertain and up to God. Because they believe the future is somewhat unclear, Latinos spend less time thinking and planning for the future. In a study conducted by the Pew Hispanic Center (2002), 42 percent of Latinos agreed that it doesn't do any good to plan for the future because one has no control over it. In the same study, only 15 percent of Anglos agreed with that statement. This Latino view of destiny is a manifestation of fatalism and since one's lot in life is already predetermined, it is somewhat futile to try to change the order of things (Chong and Baez, 2005, p. 20). This Latino view regarding destiny can be counter to that held by most Anglos who tend to believe they are in charge of their own destiny.

As you can see, the Latino cultural script about spirituality and family impacts their worldview. Organizations looking to better connect with the Latino population are well served to explore these concepts more fully. Realizing that such topics are not common items of conversation in the workplace does not lessen the obligation of organizations to attempt to grasp these concepts as a way to analyze the effectiveness of their workplace talent management programs as they relate to their Latino employee population.

SENSE OF IDENTITY

The first two categories related to the Latino cultural script reflected more on how others view Latinos. This third category focuses on how Latinos tend to view themselves. Given that approximately 40 percent of the Latinos in the United States are foreign born, adjusting to a new life and a new place to live, it is clear that a significant percentage of the Latino population is involved in an underlying cultural transition that will most definitely impact their sense of identity. Latinos tend to vary widely in the way they think about themselves. This is important for leaders to understand because it provides further evidence of the amount of diversity that exists in the Latino community. Ethnic identity, cultural identity, acculturation, and assimilation are four fundamental elements in one's sense of identity and warrant exploration by organizational leaders and Latinos, alike.

An analysis of identity patterns is incomplete without an understanding of the topics of ethnicity and race. Ethnicity is based on heritage, experience, and group membership. Ethnicity is thus related to cultural elements that can be learned and shared from one generation to the next. Some confuse ethnicity with race, but they are not the same. Race is a category based on physical characteristics such as appearance and skin color. Furthermore, everyone in the same race does not necessarily share the same ethnicity. Similarly, everyone of the same ethnicity does not necessarily share the same race.

To be clear, the terms Latino and Hispanic refer to ethnicity and not race. Being Latino involves ethnicity because it relates to the common cultural values, history, traditions, and language that Latinos share. Latinos can have a white, brown, or black skin color. It is not uncommon to meet a Latino with Spanish ancestry with blond hair and blue eyes for example. Also, some Latinos from the Spanish Caribbean islands appear to be African American because they have black skin. Although the majority of Latinos in the United States tend to have brown skin and black hair, you cannot "identify" a Latino by physical appearance alone.

Ethnic Identity

The importance that a Latino places on being seen as a Latino refers to their sense of ethnic identity and is one aspect of their social identity (Tajfel and Turner, 1986). This means that some Latinos fully embrace and are passionate about their "Latino-ness" and their Latino ethnicity is at the core of who they are. Some display this by proclaiming with great pride that they are Latino or Hispanic. Others are more passionate about their place of origin. These individuals usually prefer to be identified as Puerto Rican, Mexican, or Cuban, for example, as opposed to being identified as being Latino or Hispanic. To some, being Latino is simply an interesting fact and they neither deny their ethnic background nor do they promote it. There are also those Latinos who shy away from or even repudiate their ethnic background and prefer to be simply seen as individuals with no association to Latino group membership.

In the workplace, Latinos also have to deal with their coworkers' awareness of their ethnic identity. As mentioned earlier, because being Latino refers to ethnicity, one cannot be distinguished as being Latino simply based on language or physical appearances. This may confuse non-Latino employees when someone who does not "appear" to be Latino actually is or when someone who appears to be Latino chooses not to identify with their ethnicity. Because of this, Latinos often have to clarify or explain their ethnic background to non-Latinos. Some may chose to Anglicize their name (going by Rick instead of Enríque) or by not talking about their ethnic background in the workplace (Ferdman and Cortes, 1992, p. 271).

Cultural Identity

The sense of ethnic identity a Latino possesses is often a reflection of their cultural identity. For a Latino, cultural identity refers to their inner opinion of the features that are characteristic of the Latino group and what being a Latino implies in terms of behavior, values, and norms (Ferdman and Cortes, 1992). If a Latino believes that the characteristics associated with being Latino are positive (cultural identity), they are more likely to embrace their Latino heritage (ethnic identity). Latinos who consider the characteristics associated with the Latino population are unfavorable (cultural identity) are more likely to have an aversion to being recognized as a Latino (ethnic identity).

However, simply being Latino does not mean that one will see or notice Latino behavioral patterns that can make cultural identity a bit more challenging. Also, based on cultural perceptions, some who identify themselves as being Latino can have very different meanings of what being a Latino conveys. For example, as Ferdman and Cortes point out, "a Puerto Rican living in New York and one living in Puerto Rico may share an ethnic identity, but they could have dissimilar experiences and ways of looking at the world, with resulting differences in their cultural identities" (p. 251).

Understanding the Latinos' sense of ethnic and cultural identity is important for organizational leaders to understand because it often explains how they want others to view them. Some may want to oppose being typecast or they don't want to be associated with what they may perceive to be negative stereotypes. Some may want others to know they are Latino because they are trying to change the perception that some coworkers have about Latinos.

The key message here is that Latinos often have to deal with the added pressures of determining their sense of identity in the workplace. For some Latinos, it is a constant struggle to determine if they want to be seen more as an individual or as someone who is a member of the Latino community. Even those who downplay their Latino ethnicity because they desire to be seen more as an individual often still report difficulties blending in with Anglos (Ferdman and Cortes, 1992, p. 272). Other Latinos very much want their ethnic background to be recognized and appreciated, even if they do not want to be pigeonholed or labeled.

Companies that desire a work environment that is inclusive to people of all races, genders, and ethnicities should have modules in their leadership development programs that look at the concept of identity. Having leaders who are attuned to the issues of identity will be of great benefit for the workforces of tomorrow as companies become more diverse and increasing numbers of Latinos join the labor force.

Acculturation and Assimilation

Closely related to a Latinos sense of self-identity are the concepts of acculturation and assimilation. While some Latinos may not be familiar with these terms, they definitely experience the struggle between these two concepts almost daily. Latinos constantly feel pressure to determine how best to "fit in" with the American culture while simultaneously maintaining the ethnic heritage associated with their Latino roots (Padilla, 1980). This pressure to fit in tends to cause an internal conflict within Latinos and they try to reduce or at least stabilize this conflict by either acculturating or assimilating (Berry, 1980).

Because of the rapid growth of the Latino community and the high percentage of U.S. Latinos who are foreign born and first generation, this issue of acculturation and assimilation has become very political. Some U.S. citizens believe that Latinos should become "Americanized" and that they should adopt American customs, learn English, and live the American way of life as rapidly as possible, abandoning all aspects of their Latino heritage (Domino, 1992, p. 58). Others still believe in the melting pot analogy: that

Latinos and Anglos should blend their ethnicity to create a new definition of what it means to be American. The diversity that exists in the Latino community reflects the level to which they have acculturated to American society as depicted in Table 3.2.

Table 3.2
Latino Acculturation Segmentation

Mostly Acculturated (11% of Latinos)
Although they are mostly acculturated, Spanish is still spoken in the homes of many of these Latinos, and there is some Spanish media consumption.

Partially Acculturated American Latinos (23% of Latinos)
This group is extremely comfortable living in both worlds. They are a very young group with an inclination to purchase electronic gadgets, SUVs, and eat fast food. They are the group of Latinos most likely to be currently seeking education beyond high school (college or vocational school).

New Latino (26% of Latinos)
Relatively young, mostly foreign-born and have lived in the United States for a significant amount of time. Having family and friends close to them is very important and they prefer participating in activities where they can include the family. They tend to live in large metropolitan areas and consume a significant amount of Spanish media.

Latino Traditionals (14% of Latinos)
The oldest group. Most are foreign-born, but as a group have been living in the United States the longest. They have conservative values in terms of women's roles and religion. In general, although they have an attachment to the United States, they are uncomfortable with the American way of life.

Unacculturated or Unacculturated Stable (9% of Latinos)
Foreign-born Latinos who tend to live in areas with high concentrations of Latinos, and a large proportion are homemakers. People in this segment have no need or motivation to acculturate further. In fact, they do not feel like minorities.

Unacculturated Traditionals (17% of Latinos)
Foreign-born Latinos who have been in the United States the shortest amount of time and tend to live in key entry points. They are the youngest segment. They have close ties and keep in touch regularly with friends and family in their country of origin.

Source: Synovate. *U.S. Hispanic Market Report,* Synovate Publications, 2004.

For Latinos in the United States, acculturation refers to their ability to adopt some of the beliefs and behaviors of the dominant American culture while simultaneously holding on to their Latino heritage. As Latinos acculturate, they learn more than just the English language, they also begin to learn about American history, appreciate the significance of American holidays and navigate its idioms and jargon. Acculturation for Latinos also tends to involve reaching out to those around them to form new friendships.

However, acculturation also means that while they are learning to adapt to the American culture, Latinos still maintain a connection to their Latino heritage. Some do this by maintaining fluency in Spanish and by still embracing various aspects of their Latino cultural script. Others remain connected to their Latino heritage by keeping in touch with friends and family in their country of origin and by keeping abreast of news about their place of birth. Latino acculturation ultimately involves the progression followed as they discover more about American culture and adapting to it to function better in it while simultaneously maintaining their Latino heritage. This process ultimately alleviates some of the pressure to "fit in."

Assimilation is the other method some Latinos use to alleviate the pressure to fit in. When a Latino assimilates, they tend to adopt all of the American customs and values and to leave behind or ignore their Latino heritage. Assimilation usually results in the complete loss of their original Latino ethnicity as they become absorbed into the dominant culture. Some perceive assimilation as a conscious effort to abandon all traditional Latino values (Domino, 1992).

Some Latinos feel pressure to assimilate based on their employment status, particularly if they are the only Latino in the organization or at a certain level. For others, the need to assimilate arises if they marry into a non-Latino family, involving a necessity to change their attitudes and values for the sake of the marriage. Some Latinos may feel that their pursuit of education may exert pressure to assimilate in order to maintain academic progress. Assimilation eventually becomes evident when a Latino makes a conscious effort to become completely "American."

Some Latinos neither assimilate nor acculturate; they simply maintain all aspects of their Latino heritage and do not attempt to fit in with the American culture. These are usually first-generation Latinos who tend to shield themselves and their children from non-Latinos and things that are not Hispanic. They also are more likely to attend Latino-orientated events and only feel comfortable among other Latinos. With Latinos tending to live in areas with high concentrations of other Latinos, some of these individuals find it fairly easy to avoid assimilating or acculturating.

SUMMARY

This chapter told you more about what makes Latinos unique. Latinos vary widely in their adherence to Latino heritage and their perspective of Latino identity. It is not just the presence or absence of these items that defines Latino heritage, but rather the interconnectedness of these attributes that characterize what it means to be Latino. By exploring the Latino cultural script, you are better able to appreciate the background and experiences that create Latino identity and how it influences their outlook on family and the workplace. This chapter also highlighted how Latinos tend to be different from non-Latinos. Table 3.3 lists some of the ways Latinos tend to view things differently than Anglos. By studying such differences, you can better understand how Latino diversity can enhance work group performance if understood or how it could detract from effective work group functioning if misunderstood or misinterpreted.

By embracing these insights, organizations are better prepared to create inclusive work environments that allow Latino differences

Table 3.3
Value Differences

Latino Values	Anglo Values
Based on Catholicism, Spanish colonialism, and respect for tradition.	Based on Puritan, Protestant, and Calvinistic thinking of a new and free America.
Interdependence.	Independence.
Family first.	Me first.
Family helps family.	Helping self helps family.
Humility.	Self-expression.
Work hard.	Work smart.
Sacrifice.	Pay your dues.
Stability.	What's new? What's next?
Respect for authority.	Challenge authority.
Modesty.	Toot your horn.
God loves the poor.	God loves the rich, too.
I accept life's problems.	I solve life's problems.
Small success is good.	Big success is better.
Whatever God wants.	The sky is the limit.
I hope to achieve.	I believe I will achieve.
Give respect.	Earn respect.
What God wants.	The sky is the limit.

From Lionel Sosa, *Think and Grow Rich—A Latino Choice* (New York: Ballantine Books, 2006), p. 15. Adapted with permission.

to be appreciated and to be permitted to influence positively on their experience in and contribution to the work of the organization. To do this effectively, however, organizational leaders must convey a willingness to check their assumptions about what works and what does not in the workplace. It is only then that organizations create reciprocal, and mutually beneficial, relationships with their Latino employees. When this occurs, not only do Latinos and Latinas learn how to be more effective in the workplace, but organizations learn to adopt patterns that are typical in the Latino community to create an even more productive environment. And such an approach is at the very essence of what it means to be a diverse organization in American society.

By looking at the business case for Latino diversity, understanding key Latino metrics, and appreciating what it means to be Latino, practitioners now have the foundational knowledge to better appreciate and incorporate the practical solutions highlighted in the next three chapters to more effectively attract, retain, and develop Latino employees.

CHAPTER 4

IMPROVING LATINO RECRUITING EFFECTIVENESS

For many organizations, effectively recruiting Latino professionals is a critical goal. However, many human resource professionals are finding it difficult to tap into this pool of talent. One reason is simply that the demand for top Latino talent exceeds the supply. But a bigger problem exists for organizations: Many organizations have yet to realize that their traditional recruitment strategies do not effectively reach Latino candidates. Some of this ineffectiveness is due to the fact that Latinos often differ from their Anglo counterparts, as was highlighted in Chapter 3. Without revising current recruitment efforts and developing customized recruitment strategies specifically aimed at Latinos, organizations will continue to waste recruiting resources.

TRADITIONAL RECRUITING METHODS DO NOT WORK

There are a number of reasons why traditional recruitment strategies do not work within the Latino community. First, because of their ethnic diversity and difference in language and acculturation patterns, recruiting programs designed to appeal to a homogenous group will not reach many Latinos. For example, a job ad in a newspaper with a low Latino subscriber base is ineffective in reaching

Latino applicants. Almost half of the states in the United States have a Latino population of less than 5 percent according to the U.S. Census Bureau (2006b). Employers in these states who rely on job ads in local newspapers as a way to recruit Latino job candidates are highly unlikely to be successful.

A large number of Latinos do not know exactly how recruiting programs work. Most first- and second-generation Latinos in the United States do not possess any experience or working knowledge of how to land a job in corporate America. They have not been exposed to the traditional methods or events employers use to recruit, such as search firms, professional associations, or networking events (Hughes, 2003).

Even if they do become aware of certain recruiting programs, many Latinos may simply feel that such recruiting programs will not work for them. For example, if a Latino does not know anyone who has landed a job listed on the company's web site, they may assume that applying for jobs through a company's web site will not work for them either. Or if a Latino does not see other Latinos working at the organization, they may believe that the organization does not promote a diverse work environment and they will be less inclined to apply.

Corporate Mistakes

Organizations contribute to the ineffectiveness of their Latino recruiting programs through inadvertent mistakes. These mistakes generally result from a lack of understanding of the Latino community. It is important for organizations to audit their Latino recruitment efforts to see if such mistakes are being made. Not only do the mistakes lead to ineffective recruiting programs, they can also harm an organization's employment brand within the Latino community. Such mistakes can therefore have a long-term negative effect on

Latino recruitment efforts. Here are some of the most common mistakes made by corporations when recruiting Latinos.

Mistake 1: Poor Selection in Latino Job Fairs. With the heightened interest in Latino talent, a slew of job fairs targeting Latinos have appeared. Some focus solely on Latinos while others broaden the audience by promoting a diversity job fair. While in many cases the intention may be noble, namely to identify a diverse pool of talented job candidates, the choice of which job fairs a company should participate in often does not take into consideration the reputation of the organization putting on the job fair and that is a mistake.

Latino professionals have figured out that there are many job fair promoters looking to profit from the shortage of Latino job candidates. Because of this, there is a growing trend in the Latino community to boycott job fairs put on by professional event organizers who have no ties to the Latino community. Such organizations often use aggressive, trained salespeople to convince employers to attend their job fairs. However, the fees paid by employers to participate in these job fairs rarely go to the Latino community. Instead, the exhibitor fees and event proceeds are the event organizer's profit. Even though every organization has a right to earn a profit, there is growing concern in the Latino community that there are an increasing number of event organizers who are profiting from the job search of Latino professionals without providing any real service.

Today, Latino community leaders are encouraging Latinos to attend the job fairs put on by organizations with strong ties to the Latino community who have a reputation of supporting and giving back to Latino neighborhoods. Often these organizations are nonprofit like the Hispanic Alliance for Career Enhancement (HACE), the National Society of Hispanic MBAs (NSHMBA), or the National Society of Hispanic Professionals (NSHP) who use the proceeds from their job fairs to help fund Latino high school and college scholarships and to create professional development programs aimed at building the next generation of Latino leaders. Community leaders have been effective in encouraging Latino job seekers to be selective in what job fairs they attend and to participate in those sponsored by organizations with connections to the Latino community. These community leaders are also reaching out to employers and encouraging them to be selective in the job fairs they chose to attend.

The next time your organization receives a call to participate in a Latino job fair, ask the organizer of the event to explain their involvement in the Latino community and inquire whether any of the exhibitor or sponsor fees go toward funding scholarships or development programs aimed at supporting Latino communities or building the pipeline of future Latino talent. If an organizer of a Latino or diversity job fair is not able to be specific about how they give back to the community, consider passing on the event. Such decisions not only support the Latino community from a long-term perspective, they also will improve the employment brand of your organization.

Mistake 2: Narrow and Short-Term Focus.   Organizations truly looking to build a strong presence in the Latino community will greatly enhance their employment brand if they participate in events that help to incubate and nurture Latinos along their entire career life cycle. This means supporting programs aimed at high school and college students as well as those targeting early, mid-, and senior-level professionals (Hughes, 2003).

Unfortunately, due to limited budgets and resources, many organizations take a narrow and short-term approach by supporting only programs aimed at working Latino professionals in order to fill immediate job openings. Such programs tend to attract Latino professionals who are in the early to mid-level stage of their professional career. However, by taking such a narrow and short-term approach, companies miss the opportunity to help build the pipeline of future Latino professionals. This can be rectified by also supporting high school programs that provide scholarships to Latino students and college programs that better prepare Latinos to enter the workforce. Similarly, by focusing solely on early and mid-career Latino professionals, organizations are missing out on opportunities to recruit more experienced Latino job seekers who tend to be identified and recruited using different techniques than their less experienced counterpoints.

But the real mistake is missing out on opportunities to build trust within the Latino community. Trust is an essential component in building an effective employment brand in the Latino community (Rodriguez, 2004). Companies like Hewitt Associates are broadening their focus in order to extend their reach to Latinos who are in the early stages of their career lifecycle (see the sidebar Corporate Best Practice—Hewitt Associates). By developing proactive strategies that take a long-term recruiting approach, companies can strengthen the relationship between the employer and the Latino community.

CORPORATE BEST PRACTICE—HEWITT ASSOCIATES

Hewitt Associates, the human resources outsourcing and consulting provider, recently broadened their recruiting approach by leveraging their Community Partnership Program to help establish the Hewitt Career Center at Waukegan High School in Waukegan, Illinois. This center helps high school students identify their career interests and provides them with the resources and education necessary to make informed choices about what to do after high school graduation. The Center also provides access to technology tools for career navigation, a dedicated career counseling staff,

(continued)

and promotes partnerships with local employers to provide career inspiration. Waukegan school officials directly correlate the Hewitt Career Center with an increase in graduation rates, a reduction in student truancy, and a decreasing dropout rate.

The uniqueness of this program however is that Waukegan High School has a student population that is approximately 70 percent Latino. According to Andrés Tapia, chief officer of global diversity at Hewitt, the center not only builds the pipeline of available Latino talent in the future, it also has the added benefit of enhancing Hewitt's employment brand within the Latino community and supports the company's global corporate social responsibility efforts. Latino students who benefit from the services and resources provided at the Hewitt Career Center form a positive association with Hewitt that results in increased brand awareness and brand reputation for Hewitt in the minds of these young Latino students. Hewitt hopes that these students will remember the support provided by their organization and that they will consider a career working at Hewitt when they reach that stage of their career lifecycle. It also promotes a recruitment strategy that expands into earlier stages of the career lifecycle and gives Hewitt an early advantage in the war for the top Latino talent of the future.

Source: Robert Rodriguez, "Tapping the Hispanic Labor Pool," *HR Magazine,* 49, no. 4 (2004): 72–79.

Mistake 3: The One-Shot Approach. It is common practice for organizations to invest the portion of their recruitment budget dedicated to attracting Latino professionals toward one big recruiting program per year. This approach usually leaves no financial resources available to target Latino professionals for the remainder of the budget year. Often this one-shot approach entails having a huge presence at a national Latino career conference. This can definitely help an organization identify Latino professionals and can create an impression of dedication to the Latino community.

However, this is the wrong approach to take for those organizations looking to build a lasting reputation within the Latino community. Only those organizations with a presence at a variety of recruiting events throughout the year will truly be successful in building a healthy employment brand in the Latino community.

For example, consider the experience of a Latino professional who attends a large Latino career fair. They will most likely be impressed and probably will think favorably toward those companies who have a booth at the job fair, particularly if the job fair is organized by a nonprofit organization that gives back to the Latino community. However, if that one job fair is the only time the Latino professional comes into contact with one particular organization, his or her favorable impression of a company will soon fade.

Now compare that to the lasting impression a Latino professional will have if they consistently see an organization active in a variety of Latino recruitment and community events throughout the year. Consider the impact if that Latino professional sees an organization at a job fair, sees their jobs listed on Latino niche job boards, sees the organization hosting recruiting events at their corporate offices, sees their advertisements in publications that cater to Latino readers, and so on. Such a reoccurring and consistent presence by an organization within the Latino community will solidify that Latino professional's positive regard toward such an organization and creates an employment brand that has a long-term positive impact. As the war for Latino talent heats up, those organizations that have successfully created such a lasting impression will have a competitive advantage.

Mistake 4: Lack of Personalismo. As was highlighted in Chapter 3, *personalismo* is the tendency Latinos have toward wanting one-on-one, well-intentioned interactions with others who exhibit a personal, caring and respectful attitude. Such interactions allow both parties to convey warmth and a genuine interest in connecting and thus forms the foundation for the healthy relationships that are so important to

Latinos. Because of *personalismo,* Latinos will shy away from those individuals who too quickly bypass efforts to build a relationship. Thus, if a recruiter acts in an overly direct, no–nonsense manner and makes limited effort to connect with a candidate, a Latino will be turned off. This initial lack of display of *personalismo* is a common mistake made by recruiters who are more accustomed to dealing with Anglos who tend to prefer a cut-to-the-chase approach.

Here is a common scenario when a lack of *personalismo* hurts the Latino recruiting process. A company is attending a job fair and a Latino professional approaches the booth to show interest in the company. Upon a quick review of a resume, an Anglo recruiter determines that the individual might be a good fit for an open position. Next, instead of engaging the candidate in a longer, more meaningful conversation, the recruiter quickly encourages the candidate to go to the company's web site and apply for the position online, probably even refusing to accept the resume because their company does "everything electronically."

The recruiter feels he has successfully provided guidance to a promising Latino prospect. The Latino professional, however, interprets this interchange as a brush off and an indication that the company really is not interested in him. Why else would an organization encourage him to go to an impersonal web site to apply for a position when he is standing face-to-face with a company representative already? This mistake is happening with increasing regularity as more and more companies rely heavily on electronic application and tracking mechanisms. This is not an indication that these electronic methods are not appropriate. In many cases, they are necessary. However, recruiters that by-pass the chance to engage in *personalismo* with a Latino prospect in an effort to be more efficient often will not be very effective in encouraging Latinos to apply to their organization.

The other common scenario is the hiring manager or interviewer who is all business during a job interview with a Latino candidate. The interviewer spends very little time building rapport and getting to know the candidate, let alone allowing the candidate to get to know him or her. The Latino candidate may have a tendency to shut down during such an interview because he or she interprets this behavior as cold, harsh, and somewhat rude. The candidate will likely provide short answers and appear too shy or not really interested in the position, when in fact he or she really was interested. Latino candidates tend to be more sensitive to an approach that lacks *personalismo*.

To the interviewer, they are left with an impression of the Latino candidate that is less than impressive and they will probably not recommend hiring them and say the reason was "She (or he) didn't interview well." This mistake ends up being damaging because it does not lead to the hiring of a Latino candidate and it hurts the company's employment brand not only for this particular Latino individual, but also for others when the Latino candidate shares their negative interview experience with others in the community. Such a mistake can be avoided if an interviewer displays *personalismo*.

FOCUS ON BUILDING THE EMPLOYMENT BRAND

Employers who wish to attract Latino talent must be prepared to take a long-term approach, one that gradually establishes a solid word-of-mouth reputation and employment brand. Organizations desiring to cultivate this positive employer image within the Latino community must realize, however, that this is a course of action focused on the long-term and not a short-term task. Only an ongoing commitment to employment branding within the Latino community will deliver sustainable long-term benefits (Rodriguez, 2006b).

An employment brand is the image an organization conveys about what it is like to work for them. In essence, it provides a window into what it's like to work in and for an organization. An effective employment brand will attract even the most passive Latino prospects to an organization and predispose them to consider employment opportunities, even when they would not consider openings anywhere else. The ultimate goal is to build a strong and true employer brand that will succeed in attracting and retaining key talent.

Building a positive employer image in the Latino community helps to create a sense of urgency and an intellectual curiosity to act immediately to find out more about the organization. Truly effective employment brands within the Latino community convey the image that "Latinos who are like me work there." Besides appealing to external job candidates, overall a strong employment brand builds and reinforces the public's image of the firm's culture, work practices, management style, and growth opportunities.

Establishing such a brand within the Latino community involves three main elements. First, organizations must understand and value Latino culture. Employment branding is about reaching the right people. In order to reach Latinos, organizations have to know who Latinos are and they need to learn as much as possible about Latino culture. Second, organizations need to demonstrate that they offer valid career opportunities for advancement that are based on merit and not on ethnicity or race. Latinos are proud of their heritage, but they do not want to feel they are being hired simply because of their ethnicity. Third, and most important, an organization looking to establish a positive employment brand needs to become actively involved in the Latino community. Such efforts go a long way toward building trust and creating a foundation for a long-term employment relationship (Rodriguez, 2006b).

A word of caution is necessary, however. An employment brand will be quickly spoiled if it is not anchored in the reality of current Latino employees. A disconnect between what the employment brand promises and what is delivered will backfire. Latinos will quickly label such an employment brand as fake and it will ultimately result in driving away talented Latino professionals.

For example, if your employment brand within the Latino community promises career development, Latinos in your organization must receive bona fide career development support. A disconnect between the employment brand and the employment reality also leads to disengagement and turnover by Latinos who feel the company has not kept its employment promises.

For this reason, organizations looking to start an effective employment branding effort should first look internally to its existing Latino employees. The best channel for creating a picture of a company is through a dialogue with current Latino employees. This allows a company to anchor its employment brand with its Latino employees first. By collecting information from Latino employees about their experience, companies are able to identify employment attributes that are legitimate and resonate most powerfully with existing Latino employees (Rodriguez, 2006b).

Communication Channels

Once organizations have researched their brand and have identified a compelling message, the next step is to select the appropriate communications channel for their Latino target group. The choice of communication channel should be guided by what an organization wants to achieve. The ideal approach is to use a variety of channels (Universum Communications, 2005, p. 128).

Common communication channels include print advertisements, career fairs, television/radio, on-campus presentations, and the company web site. The key is to find the channel that resonates most with your particular Latino target audience. For example, assume that the top three ideal employment branding communication channels for Latino college graduates are internships, acquaintances employed by the company, and on-campus presentations. If the employer relies on job listings in newspapers, television/radio ads, and career fairs for this group, he will be ineffective. An investment in the wrong communication channel is detrimental to the whole Latino employment branding strategy.

Latino Candidate Experience

Organizations looking to maintain a healthy employment brand in the Latino community should consider evaluating the Latino candidate experience because this also can have an impact on a company's brand. Conduct surveys of Latinos who have applied through various recruitment channels and see what their experience was like. Did they have to speak with a dozen people to get to the right person? Was the company representative at the Latino career fair knowledgeable about Latino culture? Did the interview convey *personalismo?* How were candidates treated? Did anyone ever get back to them regarding a hiring decision? Research shows that those who have had a bad candidate experience will tell about 12 other people, thus undermining the company's brand message. Remember, it's not just what you say about your employment brand; it's also about what others say about it, particularly in the Latino community. For example, General Mills, a leading global food manufacturer based in Minneapolis, has a unique recruiting program that provides a candidate experience that makes Latino prospects feel like they are joining a family (see the sidebar Corporate Best Practice—General Mills).

Employers who focus on immediate short-term results may not achieve the diversity they seek. In fact, some organizations could potentially do more harm than good if they successfully recruit Latino workers without first creating a hospitable culture or real advancement opportunities. In such cases, word-of-mouth may work against the organization and the resulting employment brand

CORPORATE BEST PRACTICE—GENERAL MILLS

General Mills has an active college recruitment program and has established recruiting relationships with several colleges and universities across the country. These relationships help General Mills identify and hire hundreds of recent college graduates each year to fill entry and mid-level professional positions. The selection process for these positions usually involves an interview with a student candidate at their college campus as well as an interview at the General Mills headquarters before a decision is made whether to extend a job offer to a candidate. Since the top candidates are usually highly sought after by other organizations as well, it is common for the leading student prospects to have multiple job offers from other companies.

However, in order to improve their ability to hire the best Latino college students, Isaias Zamarripa, director of talent acquisition at General Mills, developed the Hispanic Re-Visit Weekend Program. All the Latinos who have recently been extended job offers are invited to come back to General Mills to spend the weekend as a guest of General Mills in Minneapolis, which is coordinated and run by the employees who are members of the General Mills Hispanic Employee Network. About 15 to 20 Latino students usually accept the invitation to participate in the weekend visit. Most participants arrive on Thursday night and they attend a networking event where they get a chance to meet each other as well as members of the General Mills Latino employee network. On Friday, all the student guests spend a day at corporate headquarters meeting with members from the various functional departments and with senior executives. This often includes the CEO of General Mills, Stephen Sanger. On Friday evening, they attend another networking event hosted by a local university. On Saturday, the student guests are taken on a tour of Minneapolis that includes visits to Latino communities. The main event, however, is the dinner on Saturday evening, usually at the home of a General Mills executive. The student guests attend, as do several members of the Latino

(continued)

employee network. However, attendance also includes several General Mill executives who come to enjoy the informal gathering and to meet the potential next generation of Latino leaders at the company.

According to Zamarripa, the event is always a great success and usually results in about a 90 percent acceptance rate of the job offers extended to the Latino students. For some students, it re-affirms their decision to join General Mills. To others, it provides a unique experience that differentiates General Mills from the competition. Students love the experience because it conveys to them that General Mills is committed to their success. It also provides them with an immediate network of other Latinos in the company.

Zamarripa states that the reason the event is hugely successful is because it focuses on two aspects that are important within the Latino community. One is the tendency for Latinos to want to form a strong personal connection with those they work with. The weekend allows the students to form strong connections with each other and with General Mill employees and executives. Additionally, the weekend visit conveys the message that the students will be joining a family if they chose to work at General Mills. The sense of family established during the weekend allows General Mills to connect with the cultural importance Latinos place on the family unit.

Recently, the Hispanic Re-Visit Weekend Program was recognized by the National Hispanic Corporate Council as a best practice in the area of Latino recruiting. But more importantly, it creates a compelling candidate experience for Latinos considering employment at General Mills.

will not help to attract more Latino professionals. By contrast, a longer-term employment brand approach will help increase the return on investment of Latino recruitment efforts.

STRATEGIES TO IMPROVE LATINO RECRUITMENT EFFECTIVENESS

With a solid understanding of the importance of creating a healthy brand in the Latino community and awareness of common mistakes made when recruiting Latinos, organizations now have the underlying knowledge necessary to develop strategies that will improve Latino recruiting effectiveness. If applied, the following 21 strategies will not only improve your ability to successfully hire more Latinos, they will enhance the employment brand of your organization within the Latino community.

Strategy 1: Educate Your Recruiters and Hiring Managers

Without some insight into the culture and behavioral characteristics of Latinos, the very people assigned to identify and bring in Latino talent often inadvertently push them away. Imagine the increased effectiveness of Latino recruitment efforts if your recruiters and hiring managers know the difference between the term Boriqua and Chicano, if they knew that Latinos tend to be somewhat shy and reserved during interviews, and that Latinos very much value their family. Having recruiters and hiring managers who possess such insight will provide a competitive advantage over other organizations where the people in charge of hiring Latino talent are still not aware of these aspects of Latino heritage. Many companies, including Darden Restaurants, Allianz Life, SuperValu, 3M, DaimlerChrysler, and Wachovia, have brought in Latino community leaders and consultants to help educate their human resource, recruiting, and hiring managers about Latino culture and to provide tips to enhance their recruiting effectiveness.

Strategy 2: Tailor Your Recruiting Messages

Even though Latinos tend to follow a similar cultural script, Latinos are still a highly diverse population with clearly defined differences between subgroups. It is critical to appreciate the elements that distinguish each subgroup because using a nonspecific approach to communicating with Latinos may be ineffective.

Once organizations realize that diversity exists within the Latino community, they can begin segmenting their recruiting practices to better fit the Latino audience they are trying to attract. For example, if recruiting in the Southwest, companies may want to have recruiting material with more of a Mexican spin. If recruiting in Florida, they may want to use more of a Cuban flair. If recruiting in New York, use material that appeals to Puerto Ricans. This segmented approach to recruitment advertising involves using the right message and communication channel according to the demographic and geographic area you are trying to reach.

Walgreens, the drugstore chain headquartered in Deerfield, Illinois, uses a segmentation approach when recruiting Latino professionals. In the past, Walgreens used to place the same employment ads on several of the local Spanish radio stations that targeted Latino listeners. However, based on insight gained from a partnership with the Hispanic Alliance for Career Enhancement (HACE), Walgreens quickly recognized that using the same ad on different radio stations simply because they were all in Spanish was ineffective. Walgreens realized that no single ad could appeal effectively to all the various Latino demographic subgroups. Instead, Walgreens segmented its recruiting targets and customized their Spanish-language ads for each radio station depending on the Latino demographic the station most appealed to. Those stations that appealed to a Mexican audience used Spanish words and jargon mostly used by Mexicans. Radio stations that catered to a Puerto Rican audience ran ads that contained background music more familiar to Puerto Ricans.

According to Tammy Napoli, director of recruitment and diversity services at Walgreens, this strategy is one that that speaks to various Latino subgroups on their own terms (Rodriguez, 2004).

Strategy 3: Leverage Latino Employee Affinity Groups

Many Latinos tend to prefer identifying jobs through their network of family and friends because they trust their judgment. For this reason, companies that have organized Latino employee affinity groups should look to these groups for referrals and to help spread the word regarding hiring opportunities within their community. Even organizations that do not have an organized affinity group of Latino employees should make their Latino employees aware of any referral programs or job opportunities.

That's what happens at Ecolab Inc., the world leader in premium commercial cleaning and sanitizing products based in Minneapolis, Minnesota. Ecolab aggressively leverages its Latino employee network and referral system to identify and attract more experienced Latino talent. Although the company has a multifaceted recruitment strategy, its employee referral program has been the "most successful" at attracting Latinos, says Sue Metcalf, vice president of recruitment and selection at Ecolab (Rodriguez, 2004).

Strategy 4: Seek Out Latino Community Leaders

Another way to raise your company's connection with this important demographic group is to seek out neighborhood and business leaders in the Latino community. Forging relationships with these leaders will serve an organization well for a couple of reasons. First, it will help an organization better comprehend and become familiar with issues unique to the Latino community. Such insights can help an organization to better position itself to serve these communities. From an employment perspective, having these Latino leaders know more about your organization and job opportunities can significantly improve a company's employment brand.

Caterpillar, the world's leading manufacturer of construction and mining equipment, reached out to Latino community leaders in Chicago to help them improve their recruitment of senior Latino professionals. Caterpillar executives held a private dinner with members of various Latino communities. During the meetings, Caterpillar shared information about their organization, about their Latino initiatives, and highlighted current job opportunities within the organization. The Latino community leaders provided advice on the Latino initiatives and educated Caterpillar on trends within the Latino community. Not only did these dinners build bridges of understanding between the members of both groups, they led directly to the hiring of several senior Latino professionals by Caterpillar. Community leaders who attended the dinner event referred some of those hired to Caterpillar. Leveraging community leaders taps into the Latino cultural aspect because community leaders are highly regarded and trusted by Latinos.

Strategy 5: Partner with Your Community Affairs Group

If your organization has a community affairs department, work with them to partner on events that are geared toward the Latino community. The Hewitt Career Center in Waukegan High School mentioned earlier in this chapter is an excellent example of the leverage an organization can get by partnering with community affairs departments. Such efforts significantly improve a company's employment brand and reputation in the community, which ultimately makes it easier to attract Latino professionals. Another unique approach could be to sponsor Latino events that help to recognize and reward Latino leaders. For example, each year the Hispanic Chamber of Commerce of Minnesota recognizes 25 Latino leaders under the age of 40 who have demonstrated significant accomplishments and a commitment back to the Latino community. These young Latino leaders are given a *"25 on the Rise"* plaque and are honored at an award dinner ceremony. Several notable employers such as McDonald's, Carlson Companies, Cargill, Wells Fargo, and others sponsor the event. The event sponsors receive the biographies of the award recipients and have an opportunity to meet them at the award dinner. The sponsoring organizations usually send members from their recruiting team to attend. Sponsoring such an event is a keen employment branding and recruiting opportunity. Sponsoring the event increases the name recognition of these firms to these young Latino leaders. Second, the sponsor organizations have an opportunity to meet bright, young Latino leaders in their local business community who can be potential job prospects for their organizations or who may refer a sponsoring organization to their friends. Unique approaches like this allow a company to differentiate itself from competitors in the Latino job market.

Strategy 6: Partner with Universities with High Latino Student Populations

Organizations looking to hire Latino college graduates into functional leadership programs should consider partnering with reputable colleges and universities with high Latino student populations to increase the likelihood that Latino graduates will consider employment with them. To start, companies may want to consider becoming more familiar with the Hispanic Association of Colleges and Universities (HACU)—the only national educational association that represents Hispanic Serving Institutions (universities where total Latino student enrollment constitutes a minimum of 25% of the total university enrollment). HACU represents over 450 schools committed to Hispanic success in higher education and its member institutions

CORPORATE BEST PRACTICE—3M COMPANY

In an effort to build the skills and capabilities of new hires going into careers in sales, 3M Company, the diversified technology company headquartered in St. Paul, Minnesota, has partnered with a handful of universities to help launch undergraduate degree programs with a concentration in sales and sales management. In 2005, 3M established a partnership with DePaul University, located in Chicago. Because 3M is looking to increase the number of Latinos who pursue careers in sales, it chose DePaul University because of its strong academic reputation and because 13 percent of DePaul's student population is Latino. 3M provides funding, sales training expertise, and guest speakers to DePaul to help with the development of the sales curriculum and with course delivery. The partnership also includes 3M internships for DePaul students enrolled in the sales program.

DePaul provides 3M the opportunity to have input on the outcomes of the sales program and on sales course content. Because of the high Latino student enrollment at DePaul, it increases the chances that a Latino student will pursue the sales educational program. The ultimate goal is to hire graduates from the sales program at DePaul into entry-level sales jobs at 3M. Graduates of the sales degree program, regardless of their race or ethnicity, will have an advantage over the competition because of the sales education they received and the sales capabilities they were able to develop during their internships with 3M. By partnering with DePaul, 3M not only has the opportunity to hire better-qualified college graduates into sales positions, the chance that these graduates are Latino is also greatly improved. 3M has had several Latino student interns and has successfully recruited Latino graduates from the program for positions. The program has been extremely successful and DePaul now has similar partnerships with several other corporations.

The approach taken by 3M is an excellent example of a company helping to build the pipeline of available Latino talent by developing programs that meet their needs in collaboration with universities with high Latino student populations. Companies wanting to increase Latino employee representation in finance, engineering, sales, human resources, or any other functional job area should consider partnering with local universities that have a significant Latino student enrollment.

together total more than two-thirds of all Latino college students. 3M successfully partnered with a Hispanic Serving Institution to help improve the recruitment of Latino sales professionals (see the sidebar Corporate Best Practice—3M Company).

Strategy 7: Affinity Job Boards

Employers using a mainstream online job board may not be reaching Latino job seekers. Latinos often are not as familiar with mainstream online job boards as they are with niche job boards that cater to the Latino population. For example, employers looking to increase the effectiveness of their Latino recruiting efforts may want to consider online job boards such as LatPro.com where 94 percent of their active registered users speak Spanish or with iHispano.com, which has a network that reaches over a million Latino professionals. Such boards not only exclusively reach Latino professionals, but using such niche sites also enhances a company's employment brand in the Latino community.

Similarly, most Latino nonprofit associations will allow companies to post job opportunities on their web sites. This provides an opportunity to list job postings on web sites visited predominantly by Latino professionals. The nonprofit association web sites of the Hispanic Alliance for Career Enhancement (HACE) or the National Society for Hispanic MBAs (NSHMBA) and many others provide an excellent opportunity to list job opportunities that will be seen by Latino professionals.

Strategy 8: Feature High-Ranking Latinos

Who is the highest ranking Latino professional at your organization? This is a question that a Latino candidate is likely to ask when considering employment at an organization. Having talented Latinos in upper-level positions sends an important message to Latino job seekers. Knowing that a company has Latinos in executive positions reinforces the potential for advancement and underscores the fact that an organization has an inclusive work culture. Featuring high-ranking Latinos in recruitment advertisements, company web sites, and sourcing events indicates to Latino job seekers that others like them can reach executive level positions in that firm.

Companies with high Latino representation at senior-level positions thus have an advantage when it comes to attracting more Latino talent. For example, Abbott Laboratories, the broad-based health care organization located in Illinois, enhances its ability to recruit top Latino talent due to the high percentage of Latinos in top positions. Latinos make up 10 percent of Abbott's corporate officers and 8 percent of the company's board of directors (Rodriguez, 2004). This last fact is particularly impressive given that Latinos represent only about 1.6 percent of the approximately 5,900 board seats at Fortune 500 corporations—and the vast amount of these corporate boards have no Latino representation—according to a study conducted by *Hispanic Business* magazine ("The U.S. Hispanic Economy in Transition," 2005). Having the Latino executives at Abbott serve as role models makes a job opportunity at Abbott much more appealing to a Latino job prospect.

Similarly, the web site for McKinsey & Company, the management consulting firm, features Luis Ubinas, a senior partner who is of Latino heritage. The web site highlights the fact that Luis grew up in New York, earned an undergraduate and MBA degree from Harvard, and that he is a member of the Hispanic/Latino consulting group at McKinsey. The web site even includes a quote from Luis in which he indicates why he believes McKinsey is a "fantastic place" for individuals of Hispanic/Latino background. Endorsements such as these from Latino employees at a company really help to make an organization more appealing to Latino candidates.

Strategy 9: Hold a Company Open House

Organizations should consider hosting a recruiting open house event for members of the Latino community as a way to enhance the name recognition of an organization, and also identify Latino talent. At such an event, the organization can provide more information about the company in general, share insights into various functional career paths taken by those at the firm, and highlight any specific positions the company is looking to fill. By sharing important information about the company, an organization can create a sense of excitement for those attending the event.

The key to such an event is getting a sufficient number of Latino professionals to attend a recruitment open house, and to make sure the *right* Latino professionals attend. A partnership with an organization that already has contacts in the Latino community will probably be necessary to promote the event as well as to invite the right Latino professionals. Target Corporation uses recruiting open houses successfully (see the sidebar Corporate Best Practice— Target Corporation).

Strategy 10: Create a Presence on College Campuses

Proactive organizations are identifying and working with the Latino leaders on college campuses to identify top talent early. This usually involves creating leadership training programs for campus leaders of the Latino student associations. Some organizations provide honors, awards, and scholarships to Latino students who demonstrate certain

CORPORATE BEST PRACTICE—TARGET CORPORATION

Target Corporation, based in Minneapolis, hosts several recruitment open house events a year specifically for Latino candidates in multiple cities throughout the country. To ensure such events are successful, Target partners with the Hispanic Alliance for Career Enhancement (HACE) to help promote the events and to assist in identifying the right Latino professionals to invite. Target open houses usually are scheduled several months in advance to allow enough time to sufficiently spread the word about the event within the Latino community.

The recruiting open house events take place after work and incorporate sufficient time for general networking between the Latino attendees and company representatives. A typical open house involves a short program during which leaders from Target talk about the history of the company, company culture, and its current financial standing. Members of the human resource department describe Target career opportunities as well as describe what characteristics they are looking for in top candidates. The part of the program that tends to have the biggest impact, however, is when current Latino employees, at various job levels within Target, share their employment experiences with the organization.

These open house events are so successful, that they create a positive buzz about the company within the Latino community. Target typically hires several Latino professionals from each event.

leadership capabilities and achieve certain grade point averages. Building such a presence at the college level is usually relatively inexpensive and allows companies to identify future Latino leaders very early. Also, such a presence augments any general college recruitment programs established by an organization (Hughes, 2003). These sponsoring organizations find it easier to recruit Latinos who already have a positive impression of the organization.

Strategy 11: Hire Inroads Interns

Inroads is a nonprofit organization that trains and develops talented minority youth for professional careers in business and industry. Young Latino students are increasingly choosing Inroads to help obtain paid, multiyear, real world professional experiences and year-round personal and professional development. For organizations, Inroads can provide early identification of talented Latino and other ethnically diverse students. Inroads also requires interns to participate in specific job readiness and leadership training. For example, some training sessions focus on how to deliver effective presentations, others on how to lead a team. The sessions often include unique areas such as how to glean information from the *Wall Street Journal* and how to play golf. Inroads interns must also maintain certain grade point average requirements to remain eligible.

Companies that partner with Inroads commit to providing a multiyear professional opportunity for an intern and to consider the intern for full-time employment after graduation. Based on the performance of the Inroads intern, organizations determine if the Latino student should receive an offer for employment upon graduation. Recent Inroads statistics indicate that nearly 90 percent of Inroads interns accepted offers for full-time employment by their sponsoring companies. Inroads thus provide an organization with a wonderful source of young Latino talent due to the work experience, training, and academic guidance received by the interns.

Strategy 12: Advertise in Latino Publications

More and more Latino-focused publications are emerging each day. Many of the ads in these publications aim to entice Latinos to purchase certain products and services. Because of the predominant Latino readership of these publications, they make for a great place for ads encouraging Latinos to consider companies for employment. Publications such as *Hispanic Magazine, Latina Magazine, Hispanic Trends, Hispanic Business,* and *Latino Leaders* target a Latino readership that covers a wide cross-section of upscale Latinos ranging from students to professionals, executives, entrepreneurs, and savvy, career-minded Latinos.

Employment-related ads offer a new way to build an emotional connection between a company and the Latino demographic group. The placement of employment ads in Latino magazines helps to build comfort, trust, and a level of familiarity among the Latino subscriber base. This is vitally important because trying to convince people to join an organization means that you are asking them to change their lives in some capacity. To make such a change requires someone to feel comfortable with the organization. Employment-related magazine ads in Latino publications help to convey that sense of comfort.

Strategy 13: Career Booth Staffs

When an organization has a booth at a Latino career fair, always try to have some Latino employees staff the booth. Organizations should engage Latino employees to work the booth, even if they are not in human resources or recruiting. Having a Latino at a career booth, especially one who speaks Spanish, almost immediately puts Latino candidates more at ease. One reason is that candidates can quickly determine that "Latinos like them" work at the organization. This might help to alleviate any concerns they may have about being the only Latino at the company. More importantly, it allows the candidate to relax a bit more knowing they are speaking with someone from a similar ethnic background. When Latino candidates feel more comfortable, they make a more favorable first impression.

Those firms that are not able to staff their Latino career booths with Latinos are at a disadvantage. The absence of any Latinos at a company booth places a question in the minds of Latino candidates (even more so if the majority of the other companies at the career fair have Latino employees at their booths). A Latino candidate may question whether the company provides a work environment that is favorable to them. Latinos assume that the people they meet at career fairs are representatives of the company. Companies that bring enthusiastic, polite, and engaging Latino employees, who are accustomed to practicing *personalismo*, will enjoy a positive word-of-mouth reputation and enhanced Latino recruiting effectiveness.

Strategy 14: Participate in Latino Career Fairs

A comprehensive strategy focused on recruiting more Latino professionals should include participation in a Latino career fair. Participation in general career fairs or diversity career fairs may not be enough if you want to reach a significant number of Latino candidates. Failure to participate in Latino career fairs places a firm at a disadvantage compared to those firms who are enhancing their employment brand in the Latino community through their participation at such Latino specific events.

The question then becomes which Latino career fairs should a firm target. As mentioned earlier in this chapter, companies should attend career fairs run by organizations that give back to the Latino community. The largest, most reputable, and generally most effective Latino career fairs targeting Latino talent are put on by two non-profit organizations—the Hispanic Alliance for Career Enhancement (HACE) and the National Society for Hispanic MBAs (NSHMBA). HACE hosts multiple career fairs each year that attract Latinos across the career continuum including entry-level, mid-level, and executive job seekers. HACE hosts their career fairs in regions with high Latino populations including Chicago, New York, Houston, and Miami and soon in Los Angeles. Along with having numerous companies in attendance at each career fair, HACE also provides development workshops for Latinos throughout the event. The HACE Latino career fairs are an excellent choice for organizations looking for educated, talented Latinos at various levels of experience and across multiple functional areas.

The NSHMBA career conference is regarded as the largest single-event Latino career fair in the country. Attendance for the multiday career fair usually reaches in the thousands with over 300 corporate and academic sponsors. Attendees tend to hold, or are seeking, MBAs and are looking for a position in business. Similar to the HACE career conferences, the NSHMBA career conferences include developmental programs for attendees, and in addition they include an award ceremony and unique events such as case competitions for current MBA students.

Both HACE and NSHMBA cater to job seekers in multiple functional areas. Companies looking to identify Latino professionals for specific functional areas should consider attending career fairs hosted by Latino associations that target those functional areas. For example, organizations looking for engineering and technical professionals should consider the career conference hosted by the Society of Hispanic Professional Engineers (SHPE). Companies looking for Latino talent specifically in accounting and finance should consider attending the career fair hosted by the Association of Latino professionals in Accounting and Finance (ALPFA). Today, there seems to be a Latino association dedicated to just about each functional area and most host a career fair of some kind. For a list of Latino functional associations and other Latino organizations, see the Appendix at the end of the book.

Strategy 15: Develop Strategic Partnerships with Latino Organizations

Companies serious about attracting Latino talent need more than transactional relationships with Latino associations. To truly achieve results, companies should form holistic and strategic relationships with Latino associations. Some companies are under the impression that simply providing a big check to a Latino association is strategic. It is not. A true strategic relationship requires executive support, a high sense of engagement by the company, and the willingness to commit both financial and people resources. Only after companies fulfill their part of a strategic partnership can they then hold Latino associations accountable for fulfilling their obligations. Unfortunately, it is common for large, multinational organizations with billions of dollars in revenue to fail to live up to their end of the strategic partnership only to hold the much smaller, nonprofit Latino association solely accountable for not delivering results.

Besides executive commitment, high engagement level and resources, one of the first questions organizations need to answer when partnering with a Latino association to help meet recruiting targets is deciding who will own the relationship within the company. Since each functional department within a company has slightly different goals and objectives, determining who will own the relationship with the Latino association is a key consideration. At some organizations, the diversity department maintains the relationship in an effort to ensure hiring practices are inclusive and result in a diverse slate of candidates that includes Latino professionals. At other companies, the recruiting arm of the human resource department maintains the relationship. When this occurs, generally the focus tends to be on identifying the most effective ways to identify, select, and hire Latino candidates for opportunities across the organization. It is also common for the community affairs department to spearhead the relationship with the Latino organization. Here, the focus is on maintaining a positive image, employment brand, and presence within the Latino community. Finally, at some firms, the relationship is established and maintained with a specific business unit. Here, the partnership tends to have a more narrow focus, namely on sourcing Latino talent for this specific business unit or geographic region. So depending on the goals of the partnership, not to mention who has the budget, determining who will be responsible for the relationship with the Latino association is critical and should involve discussions with several stakeholders within a company.

When an organization has made a commitment to act as a strategic partner and has determined which department will own the relationship, the next question becomes selecting the right Latino association to partner with to help drive hiring of Latino talent. Today, there are dozens of organizations and Latino associations that can help a company meet their goals for hiring Latino talent. Many can do so only on a transactional basis and for some companies that is all they need. The pool of organizations and Latino associations that can effectively deliver results on a strategic basis, however, is much smaller due to the size, focus, and capability required to deliver effectively.

Ultimately, each company must establish its own set of criteria for determining which Latino association or organization it will select to form a strategic partnership to help find Latino talent. Unfortunately, some companies do not consider enough criteria when making their selection. When a firm uses a limited set of criteria in choosing a partner organization, it ultimately limits the value of the partnership. Because other criteria items are not considered, it raises the possibility of overlooking a Latino association that would have made a much more logical choice for a strategic partnership. The set of criteria that a company can use is endless, the key is to develop an exhaustive list that includes items that not only impact the ability to deliver results, but also reflect the character and integrity of the Latino association. Companies that use criteria that only focus on the ability to deliver short-term results could ultimately be hurting their long-term employment brand by inadvertently choosing a Latino entity with a less then stellar reputation in the Latino community.

Companies may want to consider the approach used by the Hispanic Alliance for Career Enhancement (HACE). When in discussions with a company that is seeking a strategic partner to help identify Latino professionals, HACE proactively informs the company how they rate on a broad range of key differentiating factors as outlined in Table 4.1. Organizations can use these criteria to identify and select which Latino organization they want to support. Many organizations do not consider all of these factors at the selection phase, but they are key items to consider during the implementation stage and should not be overlooked. Using this approach allows HACE to simplify the organization's assessment process, and it also provides a broader framework for the company to use to assess other Latino associations that are also being considered.

Strategy 16: Highlight Latino Diversity on Web Site

Latinos who are considering employment with an organization will not only review the company's web site for information regarding job opportunities, they will also search for information regarding Latino diversity. Latinos will look for general information regarding the company's stand on diversity and they specifically will try to determine if a company has a Latino employee affinity group, whether the company supports Latino issues or organizations, and whether the firm has been recognized as a good corporate citizen by Latino publications or associations. Finding information that indicates a strong

Table 4.1
Nonprofit Partner Selection Criteria

Factors	HACE	Org. A	Org. B
Year-round programs	Yes		
Full-time staff to implement all programs and events	Yes		
Account manager assigned to each company	Yes		
U.S. work-authorized candidates	Yes		
National presence in key Latino regions—NY, FL, TX, IL, and CA	Yes		
Senior, mid-level, early, and entry-level candidates	Yes		
Presence at top 20 Latino university campuses	Yes		
Latino diversity training and value-added information	Yes		
Focus on candidate preparation and development	Yes		
Relationship building with companies; not transactional	Yes		
Single request for funding— No multiple asks	Yes		
Strategically focused on mission	Yes		
Lower all-in costs for conference presence	Yes		
Corporate social responsibility offering	Yes		
Scholarships—College and high school	Yes		
Measurement and tracking of results	Yes		
Stable and credentialed management	Yes		
Board governance—Inclusive, insightful, and effective	Yes		
Financial disclosure—Transparent and timely	Yes		
Proprietary research	Yes		
Operational excellence—Six sigma	Yes		
Guaranteed results	Yes		

Source: Hispanic Alliance for Career Enhancement (HACE).

sense of Latino diversity within a firm helps to raise the company's employment brand and will make the Latino candidate that much more likely to consider opportunities at the firm.

There are many examples of companies that highlight their strong commitment to diversity in general and to Latino diversity in particular. Aetna, a leading diversified health care benefits company, devotes significant space on its web site to highlight its commitment to diversity in all aspects of their business. Latinos who are reviewing the diversity information on Aetna's web site quickly will notice that the company has a Latino employee affinity group called the Aetna Hispanic Network, that the top diversity executive at Aetna is Latino, that the company partners with Hispanic Serving Institutions, and that Aetna provides training and other services in Spanish. Other information of interest to Latinos on the Aetna web site include the company's financial contribution to the Hispanics in Philanthropy association and information highlighting that the Aetna Foundation funded a video of a Spanish-language soap opera to dramatize the trials of a Hispanic family member dealing with depression. Such a Latino-orientated presence on Aetna's web site definitely impresses Latino candidates and provides Aetna with an advantage in the competition for Latino talent.

PepsiCo, the convenience food and beverage company, has a significant Latino presence on its web site. A quick tour of PepsiCo's web site reveals that the company supports a variety of Latino associations such as the Cuban American National Council, the Hispanic Association on Corporate Responsibility, the League of United Latin American Citizens, the National Hispana Leadership Institute, the Hispanic Corporate Council, the Puerto Rican Legal Defense and Education Fund, and the U.S. Hispanic Chamber of Commerce, to name a few. Latino visitors to the web site will also notice that PepsiCo has won numerous diversity awards and has been recognized for their commitment to Latino diversity. PepsiCo received a high ranking in the corporate index as measured by the Hispanic Association on Corporate Responsibility. PepsiCo was also recognized as a wonderful place to work by *Diversity Inc. Magazine, Latina Style Magazine*, and *Hispanic Magazine*.

The Latino presence on the company's web site provides an advantage to recruiters at PepsiCo and Aetna when trying to hire Latino professionals.

Strategy 17: Connect with Latino Student Associations

Maybe your organization is too small to form a strategic partnership with a university with a large Latino student population. Another approach to identifying bright, young Latino talent is to connect with various Latino student organizations across a number of colleges and universities. As more Latinos enter college, they are beginning to form a large number of Latino student associations. These associations provide a wonderful opportunity for organizations to begin supporting programs that will help build the pipeline of future Latino talent. Also, these associations present a wonderful opportunity to begin identifying top Latino prospects for internships and postgraduation hiring.

Some Latino student associations are specific to only one university or college such as the Texas A&M Hispanic Graduate Student Association or the University of Chicago Latin American Business Group. Others Latino student associations with chapters across several universities promote educational excellence for all their student members. Some of these national Latino student associations are the Hispanic Business Student Association, Latinas Unidas, National Association of Latino Fraternal Organizations, National Network of Latin American Medical Students, and the Strategic Alliance of Latino Student Associations.

Organizations can partner with these organizations in several ways. One popular approach is to sponsor an association project or program. Another approach is to ask employees to serve as mentors to the students in these associations. A company can also serve in an advisory role for the group or work closely with the faculty advisors of these associations. Organizations can also have their employees serve as guest speakers on various topics. An organization can provide scholarship or internship opportunities to Latino students. Regardless of how a company chooses to connect with the Latino student association, by taking the right approach and providing support, the partnerships with these associations help to improve a company's employment brand within the Latino community and build the pipeline for future talent.

Strategy 18: Utilize Company Alumni and College Alumni Associations

Latino alumni of an organization can be a valuable source of Latino employee referrals. Also, Latino alumni may choose to return to the company some day. If a Latino alumni employee had a positive work experience, they will not hesitate to refer Latino acquaintances to their former employer. Corporate recruiters should consider contacting former Latino employees for referrals. Companies with well-established alumni networks include Procter & Gamble, McKinsey, Microsoft, Hewlett-Packard, Deloitte Touche Tohmatsu, and Agilent Technologies.

Also, several schools now have Latino or Hispanic alumni associations. Harvard Business School recently launched its Latino alumni association whose mission is to provide postgraduate management education, networking, and career advancement opportunities for Latino alumni. Other schools with similar Latino alumni associations include Cornell, UCLA, USC, INSEAD, and Stanford to name a few. Current Latino employees who are alumni of schools with a Latino alumni association can help to attract top Latino talent.

Strategy 19: Consider Diversity Recruiting Organizations

Companies looking to add Latino executives to the top tier of management should consider reaching out to executive search firms. Several of the nation's premier executive search firms now have diversity practices that have already identified senior-level diversity executives and added them to their databases. Several of these firms also track the career progression of high-potential diversity candidates in Fortune 1000 companies.

Companies that want senior-level Latino professionals included in a slate of candidates for executive positions should seek the help of an executive search firm that either has a diversity practice or specializes in placing Latino talent. Along with helping to identify candidates, these firms can also conduct objective assessments of a company's ability to attract and hire Latino candidates based on a variety of criteria. Two executive search firms with diversity practices are Spencer Stuart and Russell Reynolds.

The executive search firm of Heidrick & Struggles has gone beyond just a general diversity practice to create a Hispanic Marketing Practice. Search professionals in the Hispanic Market Practice work with companies to understand the kind of talent they require to capitalize on the enormous and immediate growth potential that the Hispanic market offers.

There are also executive search firms that specialize in identifying Latino professionals. Spanusa is one of the leading executive search firms specializing in the recruitment of bilingual (Spanish-English) and Latino executives. Spanusa's goal is to provide their clients with the most qualified Latino candidates. The firm has a database of 40,000 Hispanic professionals. The search firms of Fresquez & Associates out of San Diego, California, and David Gomez & Associates in Chicago also have strong reputations for identifying Latino candidates for their clients.

Strategy 20: Use Latino Online Community Web Sites

Besides online job boards, there are many other technology-based initiatives that companies can use to tap into the Latino talent pool. One is to use online community web sites that cater to Latinos. QuePasa.com and MiGente.com are some of the fastest growing online communities targeting English-speaking Latinos. Membership exceeds several million Latinos. The MiGente.com web site provides tools and interactive content focused on vital issues for Latinos in the United States. The content on MiGente.com reflects the needs and interests of the Latino community and allows members of the community to provide their perspective. Many organizations now have provided a company profile to help improve name recognition within the Latino community. MiGente.com allows companies to list specific job opportunities on the web site as well.

MiGente.com also allows members to post professional profiles of themselves, making it easier for them to meet other Latino professionals with similar interests. For example, a member can simply indicate he is an engineer living in Chicago and he can quickly meet other Latinos who are also engineers living in Chicago. The networking and relationship building capabilities of the online community are attracting many recruiters who want to connect with the professional networks of these Latinos. Some companies are even creating group pages on MiGente.com where members can learn more about specific functional job areas such as sales, real estate, and human resources. These organizations are providing these group pages with useful information for the members of MiGente.com, which helps to attract potential job prospects while simultaneously enhancing their employment brand in the Latino community.

Strategy 21: Recruit Recognized Latino Leaders

Recruiters review public lists of Latinos who have received recognition as leaders in their organizations or in the community looking for prospects. For example, each year *Hispanic Business Magazine* highlights the 100 most influential Latinos in the United States. Similarly, *Latino Leaders Magazine* lists their 101 top leaders in the Latino community as well. These Latinos—most are corporate executives—are selected based on their accomplishments and their ability to inspire and motivate Latinos to advance professionally. These lists provide a "Who's Who" of Latino leaders in the country and serve as an excellent resource for companies looking to identity top Latino professionals to recruit.

Another potential source of candidates includes those in positions of leadership at Latino associations or nonprofits. These leaders tend to have strong business credentials and academic success, as well as proven leadership capabilities. The boards of directors of these organizations can also serve as possible candidates to recruit because most tend to be more senior Latinos and their board position experience provides them with strategic thinking expertise.

Also, organizations might want to consider current or past participants of Latino leadership development programs as a potential source for recruiting prospects. For example, the web site of the National Hispana Leadership Institute provides the biographies of the 20 Latinas who are participating in their four-week intensive leadership development program. These Latinas tend to have substantive professional work experience with an impressive list of accomplishments. Also provided are the biographies of alums of the program as well as information on the Latina college students who are participants or alums of their Latinas Learning to Lead Institute aimed at preparing bright Latina college students to enter their professional careers.

INTERVIEWING LATINO PROFESSIONALS

Once an organization has identified Latino candidates, extra consideration should be given to the interview process, especially if the interviewer or hiring manager is a non-Latino. Due to various aspects of the Latino culture, some answers and behaviors may be misinterpreted during the interview process. Those who are more familiar with the tendencies displayed by Latinos and well versed on Latino culture will be in a much better position to make an accurate assessment of their candidacy for a position.

Highlighting Past Accomplishments

During job interviews, Latinos often shy away from boasting about their past accomplishments or strongest attributes. Latinos are more likely to feel that such disclosure is a sign of arrogance and may down play some of their previous achievements. Part of the reason for this tendency may be a Latino's conviction that taking too much pride in an accomplishment is a sign of pretentiousness (Sosa, 1999). Also, due to Latinos collectivist mentality, they will tend to give credit to a team or group for accomplishments as opposed to taking credit for themselves.

By not proactively listing their strengths and accomplishments, and by acting somewhat humble during the interview, hiring managers may assume that the candidate did not "sell himself" well during the interview. Some have commented that Latinos have a tendency to be somewhat passive during job interviews and that they may be less inclined to "fight for the job" then their Anglo counterparts. When sensing such a dynamic, interviewers should focus on the substance of the candidate, not so much on the style he or she displays during the interview. It is not that Latino candidates do not have accomplishments they are proud of or that they are not aware of their strengths, it has more to do with the fact that public self-assessment and emphasizing your own best attributes is not typical of Latino behavior (Carr-Ruffino, 2003). A common question asked during interviews is "Tell me about your weaknesses." This too may be a difficult question for Latino candidates to answer. Not that they do not have weaknesses or are not aware of what they are, but again, these types of public self-assessments are not typical in Latino cultures.

Sharing Personal Information

Latinos are generally candid about providing insights into their character and personality. Depending on their length of time in the United States and their level of experience in formalized job interviews, Latinos may share a lot of information about their morals, family history and size, marital status, and even their age (Chong and Baez, 2005, p. 180). Latinos believe they are giving the interviewer more insight into their character and individual qualities when they share more about themselves as an individual. Latinos may believe that they would not want to work for a company that does not really know who they are and thus they will want to be very open about this. Such disclosure may unfavorably impress non-Latinos who tend to be more reserved when it comes to personal characteristics during an interview. According to Chong and Baez (2005), "failure to ask personal questions may be interpreted by the Latino interviewee as a lack of interest on the part of the organization. Interviewer should explain at the onset why the scope of their interview and personal questions are limited" (p. 180).

Simpatía

Many Latino job candidates have reported experiencing difficulty with the objective manner in which most job interviews are conducted. The difficulty is partly due to the fact that Latinos seek out harmonious relations and often consider job interviews to be simply a conversation between two people who are getting to know each other, as opposed to simply a potential job associate. If an interviewer conducts an interview in an overly formal, blunt, and cold manner, or is somewhat confrontational, they are unlike to have a meaningful interview with a Latino candidate. The Latino candidate is likely to maintain detached and will not be comfortable. Since this is not their tendency, the Latino candidate will be left with an unfavorable impression of the company. Also, the interviewer may think the Latino candidate is not a strong candidate for the role, even though he or she may have the proper credentials, based on the interview. Unfortunately, non-Latinos often have no idea that their behavior during the interview process may have been the reason for the poor interview. Since Latino candidates are likely to share their terrible experience with other Latinos, the result often mars an organization's employment brand in the Latino community.

For the job interview, it is important to try to connect with a Latino candidate. Encourage an approach that is more informal where the dialogue expands beyond just business. Because Latino job candidates often expect such an approach during an interview, they will tend to be put off if the interview is not conducted as expected. Rules regarding legal and illegal interview questions may make this somewhat challenging but non-Latino interviewers should look for topics of discussion that provide the opportunity to connect without treading into areas that are inappropriate.

Other Interview Considerations

Latinos value opportunities to gain new skills and capabilities. Therefore, a key consideration for a Latino during the selection process includes whether training and professional development opportunities are available. Because of this, organizations looking to attract more Latino job candidates should highlight any tuition reimbursement, job training, and personal/professional development programs that they offer.

Since Latinos have a great deal of respect for people who are in positions of authority, job titles have increased importance. Important sounding job titles will provide a Latino employee with a certain amount of status in their community. Job titles that convey an inferior or subordinate position, such as a Junior Sales Associate, may be a turn off to a Latino candidate. In Latin America, job titles are often used to display status and power. Because of the importance placed on titles, it is common for Latinos to seek out positions with inflated job titles that may not necessarily reflect work responsibilities (Flynn, 1994).

As highlighted in Chapter 3, Latinos tend to place great priority on their family and the ability to remain close to family. Therefore, job opportunities that might require a candidate to relocate, and thus move away from their family, may be less desirable to a Latino candidate (Bean and Tienda, 1987).

Last, interviewers should be aware that Latinos do not maintain eye contact for long periods of time. Latino interviewees will likely look at the interviewer directly for a few moments and then look away. This inability to maintain eye contact may be seen by a recruiter as a lack of self-confidence. However, it is more of symbol of respect and reflects the culture. Conversely, since Anglos tend to look steadily at people while they are speaking to them, Latinos may be intimidated by such an approach or view it as challenging or a sign of disapproval.

SUMMARY

Latinos are different from non–Latinos in a variety of ways. Because of these differences, the traditional recruitment strategies used by organizations are often not effective in reaching Latino candidates. The mistakes commonly made by organizations combined with a focus on immediate, short-term results make it easy to see why organizations are struggling to identify and attract top Latino talent. To make things worse, the use of ineffective recruiting methods result in negative word-of-mouth that work against an organization making it even more difficult to attract Latino employees.

However, implementing programs proven effective in reaching Latino candidates and focusing on the employment brand of an organization in the Latino community raise the return on investment of Latino recruiting efforts. As the demographic trend continues to show an increasing Latino identity in the United States, those who can effectively recruit Latino talent will help their organizations meet its knowledge capital needs and better prepare the organization to market to the Latino consumer market. By leveraging the recruiting strategies highlighted in this chapter, organizational leaders will help their organizations gain a competitive advantage in the marketplace.

CHAPTER 5

RETAINING LATINO EMPLOYEES

It is not uncommon for organizations to spend a great deal of time, money, and resources on recruiting Latino professionals only to lose these talented individuals because of poor retention strategies. Without a deliberate strategy in place to focus on the retention elements needed for Latino employees, employers run a high risk of losing talented individuals to the competition. While this can be said all of employees, there are some unique cultural elements related to Latinos that warrant special attention.

Latino employees are probably working with a predominantly Anglo workforce. Due to cultural differences, the work styles and preferences of Latino employees may contrast significantly from those of their coworkers. Actions and behaviors that may come naturally to Anglo employees may seem foreign or unnatural to Latino employees. Latinos may find themselves having to make more adjustments to their workplace behavior than their Anglo counterparts in order to perform effectively. The perceived necessity to modify their actions and behaviors causes some Latinos tension and undue stress, negatively affecting their performance. Those who feel significant pressure to change how they normally act in the workplace may ultimately choose to leave the organization.

The issue of Latino retention is ultimately contingent on how much organizations require Latino employees to assimilate into the workplace culture. Those organizations that require Latino employees to change without providing support will have difficulty keeping their Latino employees. However, those organizations that are successful in creating a work environment where Latino employees retain some of the behaviors unique to their Latino heritage and culture will have greater retention success. Even better, those organizations that are able to learn from their Latino employees and modify some workplace practices will be truly leveraging the richness and value that a diverse organization can provide.

Most organizational leaders are fully aware of the high cost of turnover. When companies lose an employee, it impacts the bottom line because of the cost associated with hiring replacements, training new employees, and the lower productivity of new hires. However, as identified previously in this book, the demand for top Latino talent exceeds the supply. So it creates an even bigger loss when a company is not able to retain a talented Latino employee. This chapter suggests ways to enhance the probability of greater Latino employee retention. It provides information about how some of the elements of the Latino cultural script covered in Chapter 3 play out in the workplace. This chapter provides practical suggestions to help improve the performance and retention of Latino employees.

SUPERVISOR AWARENESS

The best strategy to increase the retention of Latino employees is to educate organizational leaders and supervisors about the uniqueness of the Latino culture and how Latino employees differ from Anglo employees. Without greater awareness of the Latino culture, organizational leaders and supervisors may have difficulty building a strong connection with their Latino employees. The inability to connect with Latino employees makes it more difficult to establish trust, communicate effectively, show appreciation, motivate, and treat employees fairly. Latino employees often feel isolated because their managers do not seem to have difficulty connecting with non-Latino employees. Also, a lack of awareness and familiarity about Latino culture is likely to breed discontent on behalf of Latino employees, which often results in increased turnover.

Unfortunately, when the relevance of Latino ethnicity in the workplace is discussed, it tends to revolve around topics such as stereotypes, discrimination, and intolerance (Ferdman and Cortes, 1992). To demonstrate the value of increased managerial and supervisor awareness of Latino heritage, we revisit the topic of Latino identity that was one aspect of the Latino cultural script described in Chapter 3. Further analysis of this issue increases the level of appreciation and awareness of areas that impact Latino employees. Greater awareness should allow leaders to create work environments that lead to improved Latino employee retention.

Latino Identity Revisited

Organizational leaders need to be aware that many Latinos feel the need to modify their behaviors in order to feel accepted at work. They feel a necessity to develop familiarity with the prevalent norms of the organization in order to be successful (Ferdman and Cortes, 1992, p. 266). While the same could be said for most employees, Latinos feel a heightened need to adapt because their cultural heritage tends to be quite different than what is typically found in organizations.

Values unique to the Latino culture sometimes create situations where Latino employees feel segregated because these values are not shared by their coworkers. The values that are important to many Latinos, such as *personalismo, respeto, simpatía,* and collectivism, are often not the same things their work associates consider important. This sense of being different makes it difficult for some Latino employees to have a feeling of engagement with their workplace that tends to lead to lower productivity and increased turnover.

Ferdman and Cortes highlight that besides a potential feeling of isolation, Latinos sometimes also struggle with knowing whether their ability to embrace their ethnic identity is incompatible with being seen as an individual. If they emphasize their ethnicity, they worry they might be stereotyped. On the other hand, if they de-emphasize their ethnicity, they feel stifled (p. 272).

Latinos seek work environments where their ethnic needs will be acknowledged, accepted, and supported. Simultaneously, they want their performance as an employee to be the sole factor for recognition and reward. As more and more Latinos enter the workforce, they will become more resistant to fitting into a corporate culture that requires them to squelch their individuality or ethnicity (Carr-Ruffino, 2005, p. 11). By increasing their understanding of Latino culture, organizational leaders and supervisors might be better able to identify and help Latino employees who may be struggling to maintain their ethnic identity in the workplace.

The Latino population growth in the United States has altered the skills necessary for effective leadership of the workforces of today and tomorrow. The new skills are particularly needed in industries whose labor force and growth markets are predominantly Latino. Organizations need leaders who are better equipped to create environments that allow all employees to bring their whole self to work. However, such capabilities are only possible through supervisory training and leadership development on the topic of Latino ethnicity. As the workforce of the future takes on an increasingly Latino identity, such supervisor awareness will enhance the ability to retain top Latino talent. To help build this capability, several Latino organizations are providing workshops and training seminars aimed at raising Latino diversity awareness. Academic institutions such as Kaplan University also have leadership development courses designed specifically for those wanting to gain an increased awareness of Latino culture and to enhance their ability to lead effectively in diverse environments.

LATINO EMPLOYEE RESOURCE GROUPS

It is becoming increasingly common for Latinos to seek out other Latinos within the workplace. Connecting with others who share similar values and interests often helps Latinos overcome a feeling of isolation. By interacting with other Latinos, many develop renewed feelings of inclusion and an improved sense of belonging. This is just one of the reasons that several top organizations are encouraging their Latino employees to start Latino employee resource groups. Along with encouragement, many organizations are providing support and resources so that these groups can be established effectively and help to ensure the success of their members. With this support from their organizations, Latinos are forming such groups at a rapid pace within corporate America.

In general, employee resource groups (ERGs) tend to be initiated and chartered by employees with similar interests and common backgrounds. These self-organized groups promote career development, community outreach, networking, continuing education, and social activities for their members. But the most effective employee resource groups are those that align their goals and objectives with the business objectives of the organization. The employee resource groups of today are also actively connected and often provide council to marketing, recruiting, strategic planning, training and development, and diversity departments. Such groups benefit both the organization and the members (see the sidebar Corporate Best Practice—Wachovia Corporation).

Corporate Best Practice—Wachovia Corporation

Wachovia Corporation, one of the largest bank holding companies in the United States, has always supported employee resource networks (ERNs) because they saw the fundamental value in such groups. This support led to the establishment of dozens of separate ERNs across the country in various Wachovia business locations. However, a recent audit of their ERNs highlighted many inconsistencies in the groups. Some had poor governance practices, others were not properly funded, and not all of them had the same level of leadership support and engagement. Wachovia was concerned that such inconsistencies might force some ERNs out of existence.

This concern led to a companywide effort to redesign Wachovia's employee resource groups. The redesign would more clearly allow the ERNs to deliver on the value proposition that they provided to not only employees, but to the Wachovia organization as a whole. The Latino Employee Resource Network at Wachovia was one of the ERNs that greatly benefited from the redesign effort. As a result of the redesign, the Latino Employee Resource Network has a more clearly defined business development component where they provide counsel and insight into the Latino community to Wachovia's various banking lines of business, marketing, corporate communications, and human resources.

To help provide further insight into Wachovia's strategy and business objectives, the Latino Employee Resource Network has two sponsors. One sponsor is a member of Wachovia's Operating Committee and a direct report to Ken Thompson, Wachovia's chairman, president, and CEO. The other sponsor is a senior Latino executive at Wachovia. The co-sponsors are able to educate and guide the Latino ERN from a holistic perspective. Additionally, the co-sponsors are also able to hear firsthand the key issues impacting the Latino employees and how these employees can best be utilized to support the business.

Additionally, the Latino ERN now has an elevated learning and development focus. Recently, they hosted a panel consisting of senior executives, both Latinos and non-Latinos, who shared their experiences with the group on how they became leaders and what it takes to succeed within Wachovia. Members of the Latino ERN also serve on panels so they can help educate and inform others. An example is the panel session they held on the issue of immigration and its impact on the Latino community, Wachovia's business interests, and society as a whole. The leaders of the Latino ERN also benefit from enhanced leadership development programs designed specifically for the leaders of the various ERNs to improve their professional leadership capabilities and their ability to lead their ERNs. The Latino ERN members also benefit from regional and enterprisewide events designed to bring members of the various ERNs together to share best practices, exchange ideas, and to network.

Rosie Saez, director of Wachovia's Leadership Practices Group and the lead architect of the ERN redesign effort, states, "We don't want our Latino employees to feel like they have to assimilate in order to fit in at Wachovia. Our Latino ERN allows members to celebrate who they are and also helps them value and appreciate the diversity that exists within the Latino community. More importantly, it allows our Latino employees to feel like they have a second family at Wachovia because we show that we care about them as individuals, that we want to help them to be leaders and that they are a critical part of Wachovia's business success."

Because of their collectivist tendencies, Latino employee resource groups often begin with a desire to pool thoughts, ideas, and resources in order to better support their interests. These interests usually include a desire to improve their community and their families. Other common goals include professional development and career advancement. However, before considering whether to establish an employee resource group, Latino employees want to know that their efforts will be supported. That is why it is critical that organizations appreciate and endorse the initiative displayed by those Latino employees who become involved in starting such a group. When companies support the formation of Latino employee resource groups, it sends a signal to Latino employees that the organization is sensitive to their issues, has an interest in fostering an environment of work inclusion, and want to provide opportunities for Latinos to fully contribute to the organization's success.

Latino employee resource groups can be a beneficial resource to a company because they promote employee retention. To help ensure their success, employers should consider providing tools and resources not only during the formation stage of these groups, but throughout their existence. The type, size, and scope of the potential resources that can be provided are endless, but some of the resources most commonly provided by employers are outlined next.

Self-Assessment Tools

Common resources provided by organizations to their Latino employee resource groups include access to popular behavioral, personality, or career assessment tools. Such instruments help Latino employees better understand themselves and their behavioral tendencies. Knowing more about themselves better prepares Latino employees to appreciate their own style, but also the styles of others and thus enables them to use differences more constructively. Employers often provide these tools to enable their employees to better understand their strengths, preparing them to look for opportunities to use those strengths for more successful functioning in work and life. Employees can also use the added insights gained from such tools to identify jobs that may be more satisfying based on their interests and tendencies.

Career Planning Support

Employers also often hold career planning sessions with employee resource groups. Such sessions allow Latino employees to learn more about the different career paths possible within an organization and the skills, capabilities, and experience necessary to obtain those positions. Some employers offer their Latino employees tips on how to network more effectively, how to obtain additional college education or advanced degrees, and how to create professional development plans. Access to this type of information results in Latino employees feeling much more knowledgeable and comfortable about the career opportunities that are possible within a company. By providing career planning support, companies not only help to improve retention, they also help to fill the pipeline with internal Latino talent. Career planning support can better position Latino professionals to advance their careers and assume positions of greater responsibility, visibility, and authority within the company.

Employee Orientation and On-Boarding

Because the demand for top Latino talent exceeds the supply, organizations often make great efforts to identify, attract, and hire leading Latino professionals to help ensure that employees' experience from day one is positive. Companies often provide information to Latino employee resource groups that they can leverage to help with the on-boarding of new Latino professionals. Latino employee resource groups can develop a brochure about their group to provide in the orientation packets of all new employees. At Abbott Laboratories, the Latino employee resource group, called LA VOICE, includes a pamphlet about their group in all new hire packages. The pamphlet shares information about the vision/mission of the group, the benefits of joining, information about past activities sponsored by the group, a listing of the committees that exist within the group, contact information for group leaders, details on how to become a member, and a link to the LA VOICE internal web page that contains additional information. "Having Latino employees know right away about the existence of LA VOICE immediately excites many of our new Latino employees because of the opportunity it provides to join a community of those like them," says Lisa Rodriguez, manager of corporate talent acquisition at Abbott.

Leadership Development

Members of Latino employee resource groups enhance their leadership capabilities as they manage their groups. But employers can provide additional opportunities to enhance the leadership capabilities of their Latino employees. At Abbott, members of LA VOICE participate in "Lunch and Learn" programs focused on performance excellence and a series of breakfast events with leaders in the Latino community. Aetna, the insurance and employee benefit company based in Hartford, Connecticut, often has members of their Aetna Hispanic Network participate in their "Diverse Discoveries" program that provides leadership development training for Latinos, and others, who are mid-level in the organization, are strong performers, and who have demonstrated potential for additional responsibilities and larger leadership roles at Aetna.

In 2007, Aetna also sponsored a Hispanic Network Leadership Summit with Latino employee resource groups at other organizations in the Hartford, Connecticut, area as another way to enhance the leadership ability of their network members and to allow them to meet Latinos in other organizations. The summit also provided leadership development offerings and included an inspirational session led by Charles Patrick Garcia, a highly decorated military officer, entrepreneur, author, presidential advisor, and winner of numerous awards and accolades. Aetna also encourages and supports members of the Aetna Hispanic Network to participate in other regional, national, and international Latino symposiums, conferences, and training.

Latino employee resource groups benefit from development programs, but they also can provide training for non-Latinos within the company. Latino employee resource groups often lead or sponsor sessions designed to enhance the level of understanding of the Latino community to members of their executive teams and leaders of functional departments. At Darden, the restaurant company located in Orlando, Florida, members of the Latino employee network sponsored a session with leaders of their human resource and operations groups to learn more about the Latino community and what Darden could do to more effectively recruit, develop, and retain Latino professionals. Similarly, the Latino employee network group at Dow Chemical Corporation brought in a Latino consultant with expertise on how Latinos and Anglos communicate differently. Along with leading culturally focused events, Latino employee resource groups often lead programs designed to help fellow employees learn Spanish thus enhancing the bilingual capabilities within an organization.

Group Start-Up Support

Organizations can have an immediate impact on the success of a Latino employee resource group by providing tips and resources to help the group start up. They can provide tips on how to develop a group charter, how to establish a vision and/or mission for the group, advice on what should be the structure of the group, how to establish a budget for the group, and how to select the leaders of the organization. Dow Chemical, the diversified chemical company based in Midland, Michigan, has worked jointly with their Latino employee resource group to help provide structure for the group (see the sidebar Corporate Best Practice—Dow Chemical Company).

Corporate Best Practice—Dow Chemical Company

Dow's Hispanic Latin Network has over 550 active members with six chapters covering Dow's major U.S. sites and business offices. Dow supports the Hispanic Latin Network because they believe the group is a catalyst in helping the company create a more inclusive work environment and a people-centric performance culture, both of which are key elements in Dow's business strategy.

Part of the support that Dow provides the Hispanic Latin Network includes access to individuals who play a key role in the success of the network. For example, the director of global diversity and inclusion at Dow provides the Hispanic Latin Network with their annual operating budget and works with them to ensure their operations are consistent with those of the other employee networks at Dow. The director also serves as an advisor to the network on topics related to diversity and inclusion and, when possible, shares internal and external benchmark data with the network.

Dow also assigns a management sponsor to the Hispanic Latin Network who provides operating direction and clarification of Dow's corporate goals. The management sponsor serves as a liaison between the Hispanic Latin Network and the Office of the Chief Executive (OCE), Dow's executive leadership team. The management sponsor keeps the OCE informed of the Hispanic Latin Network activities and, when necessary, solicits OCE members to serve as corporate champions on issues important to the network.

Additionally, Dow designates two internal consultants to work with the Hispanic Latin Network who not only actively participate in the network, but who also help the network with the development of strategy and communication documents.

The leaders of the Hispanic Latin Network also receive support through their inclusion on the Employee Network Leadership Team (ENLT) which is comprised of representatives from each of the Dow supported networks. The ENLT meets quarterly to review annual activities, share best practices, and identify opportunities for collaboration across functions, businesses, and geographies.

> The mission of the Hispanic Latin Network is to leverage Hispanic-Latin diversity and culture to enhance success at Dow. By providing such a high level of support to the Hispanic Latin Network, Dow not only helps the network work toward achieving its mission, it also encourages Latino employee retention and drives Dow's business strategy.

Along with providing support on the formal aspects of group formation, organizations should also provide advice on how the Latino employee resource group should address issues and challenges that commonly arise for similar ERNs. For example, the organization can provide advice on how the organization should address issues related to cultural barriers that may be experienced by members, nonmembers, and possibly even management that could prove to be detrimental to group success. Additionally, the organization could provide advice on how to increase group membership, how to partner with other groups, and how to keep the group focused on its mission. Since it is likely that several members of the group may not have had previous experience in the formation of such a group, support like this is often extremely critical.

Executive Sponsorship

Probably the best resource that an organization can provide a Latino employee resource group is to assign a member of senior management to sponsor the group. Having a sponsor serves as formal acknowledgment that the Latino employee resource group is sanctioned and supported by the organization. An executive sponsor helps to give credibility to the group and raises their level of visibility within the company. An executive sponsor is also often able to assist the Latino employee resource group in gaining access to financial resources and budget support.

Of equal importance is the role that the executive sponsor can play in helping the Latino employee resource group establish a strategy and group priorities that are aligned with those of the organization. This alignment is very important because it helps to demonstrate that not only can the Latino resource group benefit its members, it also can play a role in helping the company achieve its goals and business objectives. By sponsoring a Latino employee resource group, an executive is able to connect the members of the group to core business processes and key initiatives. This connection mobilizes Latino employee resource groups as resources to major business initiatives while at the same time broadening their business experience.

Executive sponsorship of Latino employee resource groups also demonstrates commitment and accountability on the part of the executive. At PepsiCo, each of the CEO's direct reports is responsible for the growth and development of a different group of employees. The executive who sponsors the Latino employee population is accountable for understanding the workplace issues that Latinos face. The executive sponsor works to identify the top Latino leaders in the organization and often serves as their voice to the rest of the executive committee and the CEO (Rodriguez, 2006c, p. 59). Each year, the executive sponsor of the Latino employee group shares with the rest of the committee the biggest concerns of the Latino employees, identifies the support needed by Latinos, and articulates their plans to address the concerns faced by their Latino employees. Such executive support ensures that Latinos are not left behind and that they are equally represented at the executive table.

At other companies, the executive sponsor helps link Latino employee resource groups to those within the organization who have the most need of their cultural insights. For example, with the help of their executive sponsor, the Latino employee resource group at Allianz Life, the life insurance company based in Minneapolis, Minnesota, recently was able to help the company meet some of their business objectives. Allianz Life had set a strategy to attract more Latino life insurance policyholders but their initial attempts to reach this consumer group were unsuccessful. The executive sponsor linked up the Latino employee resource group with the managers of the sales organization. Based on their knowledge of the Latino community, the group was able to pinpoint some aggressive sales techniques that were ineffective with Latino consumers. They advised the sales managers that a focus on building a relationship with Latino consumers first (*personalismo*) would produce more positive sales results—and it did. Additionally, they worked with the sales managers and with the human resource organization to more effectively recruit bilingual Latino sales representatives. They also helped the sales organization identify a leader in the Latino community who had expertise on the Latino consumer market. By assigning an executive sponsor who could connect the Latino employee network group and those who had a business need for their expertise, Allianz Life created a positive experience not only for the members of the Latino ERN, but also for the business as a whole.

As a group, Latinos tend to define success in terms much broader than simply career advancement. Success for Latinos tends to include an ability to serve their community and their family. Latino employee resource networks help Latinos achieve this broader definition of success. Also, Latino employee resource networks help Latinos celebrate their differences. This celebration helps eliminate the defensiveness and isolation often experienced by Latinos and results in greater Latino employee retention. Latino employee resource groups promote the exploration of new knowledge by inviting Latinos to share their realities, values, and concerns with others. As Latino voices enter the conversation, new ways of seeing and understanding the business world emerge.

TEAMWORK

As mentioned in Chapter 3, Latinos tend to have a collectivist mindset: they place emphasis on the needs and goals of the group before that of an individual. Because Latinos place a high value on belonging to a group, they tend to be very comfortable functioning in groups (Carr-Ruffino, 2003, p. 362). With this insight, organizations can improve employee retention by making Latinos valuable members of a team, as opposed to individual contributors.

For Latinos, being a part of a group helps provide a sense of belonging and fellowship. Latinos also tend to flourish when placed in groups where group members are dependent on one another to accomplish a goal. This interdependence helps to create a sense of community—something that Latinos tend to favor. The collectivist disposition of most Latinos also pushes them to gain commitment to a unified goal within the group, thus helping to promote greater team effectiveness.

Latinos often believe that their moral worth can be judged by how much they sacrifice in the name of the group. Thus, group assignments provide a greater opportunity for "virtue." This also explains why Latinos will go to great lengths to demonstrate their concerns for the group and feel a heightened sense of responsibility for resolving group problems. Group assignments therefore help provide a sense of purpose that many Latinos desire in the workplace. Latinos also tend to take fewer individual risks. Being in groups encourages more risk taking since the risk is shared with other members of the group (Elvira and Davila, 2005, p. 17).

Organizations benefit from Latino collectivist orientations because Latinos often provide diversity in the group. As more and more Latinos join the workforce and become part of work groups and teams, they are able to bring a variety of ideas, values, perspectives, and talents to the group. This diversity allows the group to learn from one another which strengthens the entire group.

As mentioned earlier in the book, organizations looking to promote their Latino diversity should consider developing reward systems that benefit group performance over that of the individual. The opportunity to influence rewards that result in gains for the entire group can be very motivating to Latino employees because it plays on their desire to create a sense of collective spirit (Chong and Baez, 2005, p. 37). So strong are the desires for group rewards that, in some instances, financial compensation differentials given to a single employee may result in that person being seen as a "special" member and could result in rejection by their Latino peers (Diaz-Saenz and Witherspoon, 2000).

By acknowledging Latino collectivism tendencies and creating opportunities to increase the level of group and team involvement, organizations are developing work environments that tap into Latino cultural strengths. Being encouraged to leverage their strengths often results in increased productivity and higher job satisfaction. This benefits the employer through the existence of high-performing teams but also through increased retention of Latino talent.

EMPLOYEE RELOCATION

Because of the Latino emphasis on the family unit, relocation can be an issue with Latinos. It is common for organizations to have career paths and developmental experiences that require an employee to relocate to another part of the country or to complete an international assignment. The rationale for such experiences are quite sound in that they often provide an employee with a broader perspective of the organization and consumer base. However, employers should prepare themselves for the probability that some young, high-potential Latino professionals may reject such opportunities because relocation forces them to move away from their family. Latinos are more likely to pass on opportunities that help to create career success if such success comes at the expense of family. To some

Latinos, no potential career benefit will outweigh the disadvantage they will experience by sacrificing the family value system.

For employers, relocation decisions often focus mostly on housing and moving of household goods. Organizations that truly understand their Latino workforce will realize that for Latinos, closeness to family often has a much higher priority. This added sensitivity can create a big difference when having a discussion with Latino employees about possible relocation assignments.

Organizations should consider identifying Latinos who have had successful relocation experiences and have them become a resource to Latinos who are considering a relocation assignment. The ability to connect with other Latinos who have successfully relocated and maintained positive connections with their family can be quite reassuring.

Employers often provide support regarding educational needs for children and advice on how to maintain a healthy marriage during a relocation assignment. For Latino professionals, such support should be expanded to help prepare them for all the adjustments that lie ahead regarding the connection to the extended family unit, including the shift in the dynamics of interaction with their family members. Employers should also consider providing support should the Latino employee feel some loss of self-esteem due to the inability to work and maintain a close relationship with the extended family, which can include taking care of elderly parents.

By no means should employers stop asking Latinos to relocate simply due to family considerations. However, proactive organizations should look for ways to create additional support for relocation of Latino professionals. For example, maybe employees can participate in partial relocation programs where the employees are not required to relocate completely, but instead are able to maintain their current home so that such moves seem more temporary and not permanent. Another solution would be to provide additional resources and time so that Latino employees can return home more often to help lessen the impact of being away from family.

The decision to relocate is never an easy decision for any employee. However, due to their Latino cultural script, the decision tends to be more challenging for Latinos. Some employees might feel that relocation requires them to make a choice between their career aspirations and their family. To lessen this conflict, Latinos may choose to not relocate which could hurt their chances of career success within the organization. This could result in a search to identify another employer who may not require relocation. To prevent the loss of Latino talent, companies should reexamine their employee relocation programs from the Latino employee's point of view. Such an approach could result in higher Latino professional retention.

LANGUAGE

Many Latino employees are hired specifically for their ability to speak Spanish. Often the Spanish-speaking ability of Latinos helps in sales and support of Spanish-speaking clients. However, as more Spanish-speaking Latinos enter the workforce and the work environment becomes more diverse, some companies are creating "English-Only" rules in the workplace. Such rules ban employees from speaking any language other than English at all times in the workplace including lunch and breaks. These companies believe that the use of language other than English in the workplace does not help to promote harmony in the workplace.

The Equal Employment Opportunity Commission (EEOC) has observed an increasing trend in English-only charge filings in the past few years. The result of these cases has been mixed. Those cases in which a ruling was made in favor of the employer include situations where the use of another language introduced safety concerns, limited customer interaction requirements, or other significant business concerns. In some cases, where employees have been bilingual, English-only rules have not been considered discriminatory if the employee is able to communicate in English.

However, in many cases, claims related to English-only rules have been found in favor of the employee. Employers in those cases have not been able to demonstrate a legitimate business reason for such rules. Also, English-only rules, rather than promoting harmony, have led to a disruption in the workplace. English-only rules may constitute disparate treatment against Latino employees, which is a violation of Title VII of the Civil Rights Act.

When Latino employees are not permitted to speak Spanish at work, it enhances their feeling of alienation and inadequacy. The message sent by employers who try to enforce these rules is that Latinos are second-class citizens. Such rules are especially problematic for first-generation Latinos who feel more comfortable speaking Spanish with other Latinos.

The Spanish language is a significant component to Latino identity. For Latinos, speaking Spanish provides a sense of solidarity. But to non-Spanish speaking coworkers, Spanish can lead to divisiveness. Chong and Baez (2005) point out that when Latinos speak Spanish with each other at work, it can create distrust and animosity in non-Spanish speaking coworkers. These coworkers may consider it impolite or inappropriate for Spanish to be spoken because it excludes them. Those who do not understand the language may feel they are being talked about or made fun of (p. 62).

As more and more Latinos join the workforce, language preferences could result in escalating tension between Latinos and non-Latinos. In most situations, the Latino desire to want to promote *simpatía* will push them to speak more English at work in order to avoid conflict. But not being able to converse with each other in the manner they are most comfortable with could result in Latino resentment toward the organization. This inability to bring their "whole self" to the workplace could result in increased Latino employee turnover. To help prevent this, organizations should create inclusive environments that encourage the celebration of differences. If situations occur where speaking Spanish is a problem, organizational leaders should intervene and facilitate discussion to help promote a resolution of the problem. These steps should help in Latino employee retention.

RELIGION

Latinos tend to be culturally attached to their religion. Because of this, Latinos often feel a strong obligation to attend religious events. This sense of obligation tends to be especially strong for first-generation Latinos who want to maintain a sense of continuity to the religious customs they followed in their country of origin. Religious obligations may impact Latino employee attendance at work. Some Latinos may miss work to attend religious events. As stated in Chapter 3, Latinos tend to meet their religious obligations enthusiastically because it demonstrates the strength of their faith.

Employers looking to enhance Latino employee retention should consider a stronger level of acceptance of Latino employee religious obligations. In the workplace, acceptance often takes the form of accommodation. Increasing workplace flexibility to allow Latinos to meet their religious obligations often is reciprocated with a stronger sense of loyalty to the employer. When such flexibility is provided, Latinos will make extra efforts to make up missed work by coming in on off days, coming into work earlier, or staying beyond the end of their normal workday.

But workplace accommodations are only partial solutions when it comes to Latino religion and the topic of retention. Latino employees do not want to check their spirituality at the door when they show up for work. Latinos with strong religious beliefs want to feel a connection between the values they express in their personal life and the values they are allowed to express at the workplace. Some Latinos want to bring their life and their livelihood closer together.

This desire to bring their spirituality into the workplace does not mean Latinos will pressure coworkers to pursue similar religious beliefs. Rather, it is a desire for greater integration between personal lives and work lives. When successful in combining the two, Latinos gain a sense of wholeness, work provides more meaning and a positive contribution to their lives.

If employers ignore this desire on the behalf of some of their Latino employees, some employees may lose interest in their work. Their work will simply become a means for providing a livelihood. When work fails to provide meaning to Latino employees, the result is often a sense of emptiness. If religion is not allowed to be a topic of discussion in the workplace, some Latinos will remain detached (Chong and Baez, 2005, p. 16).

The aspects of spirituality at work and religious accommodations are still relatively new concepts for corporate America. However, as more and more Latinos join the workforce, many of them with strong religious convictions, employers will have to look for more effective ways to prohibit workplace discrimination based on religion. Employers should consider having external speakers talk about religious diversity or sponsor events that promote cultural and religious tolerance and understanding. Other considerations could include adding modules about religion to diversity training programs for managers.

Managers should reassure Latino employees that discrimination based on religion will not be tolerated. Managers should also make sure to prohibit exclusive language and jokes targeted toward a person's faith or ethnicity. Avoid setting major deadlines that conflict with religious holidays. Last, managers should provide opportunities for dialogue about and awareness of religious and Latino cultural diversity. Taking a proactive stance regarding religion and spirituality in the workplace should also enhance the probability of increased Latino employee retention.

COMMUNICATION

The ability of a manager to communicate effectively with Latino employees is also a key determining factor in employee retention. But effective communication with Latino employees does not mean an ability to speak Spanish; in fact, many Latinos do not speak Spanish. Effective communications involves the broader ability for managers to take into account cultural tendencies when trying to build healthy relationships with their Latino employees. If successful in doing so, managers can help their Latino employees feel understood and respected. The following cultural elements are explored in more detail as a reference for managers to communicate more effectively with the Latino employee population.

Personalismo

Latinos want their managers to show interest in them as individuals, not just as employees. They often have an expectation that their managers will be warm, friendly, and take an active interest in their personal lives. This may be somewhat challenging to Anglo managers who may be more accustomed to maintaining a separation between business and personal matters.

Latinos readily interject their personal lives into their workplace conversations and will frequently disclose matters that others may believe should remain private. Such disclosure is a Latino manifestation of their desire to connect with their managers on a personal level. Similarly, Latino managers will often show concern for the personal and family matters of their employees. Such concern is not intended to be an intrusion; it is simply a way that some Latinos managers show concern for their direct reports (Carr-Ruffino, 2003, p. 364).

A failure on the part of a manager to try to build a personal connection with their Latino employees may be wounding, insulting, and convey insensitivity. When these behaviors are perceived, it makes it difficult to form productive relationships. Also, such behaviors create an obstacle to building trust and mutual respect. By displaying *personalismo* and showing a genuine interest in getting to know their Latino employees, managers can enhance Latino employee retention.

Conflict Management

Because *simpatía* is part of their cultural script, Latinos are likely to try to avoid conflict in the workplace. Latinos often see conflict as taking attention away from what is really important, namely maintaining harmony in the workplace. To a Latino, conflict simply polarizes people and results in a win/lose mentality.

Conflict in the workplace also leads to internal conflict within Latinos because it pushes them toward behaviors that are not in alignment with their values. Closely related to avoiding conflict is the discomfort Latinos feel when their supervisors tend to be too confrontational or "in your face." Thus, if conflict and confrontation are regular aspects of a work environment or is part of the organizational culture, it likely will result in high Latino employee turnover.

Supervisors need to understand that Latino employees prefer to avoid conflict. When conflicts arise, Latinos may have a tendency to feel responsible and this often leads to feelings of guilt because they perceive conflict as an obstacle toward maintaining healthy relationships. Because of these feelings, managers should show concern, empathy, and a sense of compassion during conflict situations.

Instead of seeing an inclination to avoid conflict as a weakness, managers may benefit from seeing it as a strength. Viewed this way, supervisors are better able to harness a Latino's tendency toward *simpatía* to help build consensus among conflicting viewpoints and to act as a catalyst toward reaching agreement.

A manager can also help a Latino employee realize that some conflict in the workplace is not always a bad thing and that healthy conflict can be productive. Because Latinos tend to place emphasis on things that support the collective group, managers can highlight how conflict handled constructively can improve group performance. Managers can also point out that an unwillingness to participate in conflict situations occasionally makes it difficult to accomplish things that are important to the Latino community. Most importantly, a manager should highlight that when conflict arises it does not necessarily mean an attack on an individual and should not be taken personally.

Conflict in the workplace is inevitable. Therefore, the more a manager can do to help a Latino employee who is uncomfortable with conflict, the better the chances are of allowing that employee to be successful. By helping a Latino employee feel more comfortable at work and by placing them in situations that play to their cultural strengths, managers help to improve Latino employee retention.

Performance Evaluations

The allocation of rewards to employees can be controversial if performance appraisals are used as the basis for such decisions. This is because performance appraisals are often ineffective because of a cultural tendency to avoid conflict between an employee and their supervisor (Osland, de Franco, and Osland, 1999). Because performance appraisals are seen as divisive in nature, they are utilized infrequently in Latin America (Elvira and Davila, 2005, p. 16).

U.S. managers may want to be aware of this problem when doing performance evaluations with their Latino employees. Instead of seeing performance appraisals as a way to clarify expectations and provide an opportunity for managers and employees to share ideas and information, Latinos may view them differently. Latinos may view performance appraisals as a way to place them in the uncomfortable position of being judged by someone else. Also, because Latinos tend to focus on the needs and performance of the group, they find feedback based on their individual performance somewhat puzzling.

Latinos have a tendency to want others to like them (*simpatía*). That is why Latinos often have a difficult time accepting criticism or constructive feedback. They will be more inclined to take feedback personally. Since Latinos tend to look up to their supervisors (*respeto*) and have worked hard to develop a personal connection with them (*personalismo*), they may perceive constructive criticism from their supervisor as being rather cruel and unkind. Because Latinos also tend to believe that they are hard workers, some may experience confusion as to why their shortcomings would be noted.

Also, even though a Latino may find such a review difficult to accept, they most likely will not challenge the assessment.

Some managers view performance appraisals as an opportunity to request feedback from their Latino employees on their performance as a manager. Such situations are considered by non-Latino managers as a chance to identify areas that they can improve upon. However, because of the respect usually given by Latinos to those in positions of authority, it is unlikely that a Latino employee will suggest areas for improvement. Much like Latinos are unaccustomed to someone pointing out their flaws, they are unaccustomed to pointing out the flaws of others, especially their supervisor. Avoiding situations that can lead to perceived criticism is another way for a Latino to maintain *simpatía*.

Performance appraisals can be awkward for any manager who is not prepared. However, when delivering performance appraisal feedback to a Latino employee, non-Latino managers should take extra care to properly prepare themselves due to the cultural elements involved. Managers should try to focus on being descriptive during such discussions as opposed to being evaluative. Also, managers should try to emphasize that such feedback are ideas that should be used to improve future performance, as opposed to criticizing past performance. An even better approach is for managers to highlight that such feedback will improve their ability to support group goals, thus linking into a Latino's collectivist desires.

In their best-selling book, "*First, Break All the Rules*" Marcus Buckingham and Curt Coffman, two consultants for the Gallup Organization, highlight that employees don't leave their employers, they leave their supervisors; and that an employee's relationship with their supervisor is the biggest determinant in their level of engagement (1999). By taking into consideration cultural viewpoints regarding performance appraisals, managers can enhance their effectiveness when applied to Latino employees. Such an approach will allow performance appraisals to be used as a mechanism to strengthen the relationship between a Latino employee and his or her supervisor. The strength of the Latino employee/supervisor relationship can thus serve as a mechanism to enhance a Latino employee's propensity to stay with an organization.

FAMILY

Since family serves as the number one priority for Latinos, a better understanding of how to embrace a Latino's sense of family can help improve retention. Employers who recognize the role that family plays in the lives of Latinos are better able to accept cultural actions and behaviors that demonstrate that tending to the needs of the family is paramount.

For Latinos, missing out on important family events and milestones can harm their relationships with loved ones. Attendance at family events such as weddings, baptisms, First Holy Communions, and graduations is extremely important to most Latinos. When work demands require a Latino to miss such an event, it can make concentration on the job difficult. If consistent work demands require a Latino to sacrifice family obligations, it may lead him or her to pursue another job opportunity. Some Latinos may pass up promising career opportunities because they feel it is too difficult to disregard the needs of their family.

Latino friendly employers should work toward creating an environment where employees do not feel that they have to choose between their family and their work. There are numerous programs that employers can implement to help their Latino employees maintain a healthy work-life balance. Such programs help relieve the stress of Latino employees because it prevents them from neglecting family responsibilities. Also, an emphasis on work accomplished, and not time in the office, will allow Latinos who diligently finish their work in an efficient manner to spend extra time with their families.

A Latino's connection to family should also be leveraged in other ways. For example, Latino employee work accomplishments and recognitions should be shared with their family members. Because of the close-knit nature of Latinos, families often feel revered and have a sense of pride when such recognition is received. Also, companies should provide opportunities that allow Latinos to bring their families into the workplace to see where they work. Extending such opportunities is usually greatly appreciated. Organizations should also consider providing rewards and recognition that support the family.

Employers can design work environments that make Latinos want to stay when their family priorities are taken into consideration. This helps to create an exchange relationship between a Latino employee and the company. By providing an environment that enriches their lives, companies are able to earn Latino loyalty every day and this often results in increased productivity and improved retention.

Summary

Once Latinos are hired, the battle in the war for talent shifts from acquisition to retention. Unfortunately, at some organizations, Latino employees are appreciated only after they have left the company. Effective retention of Latino employees requires more than just the involvement of the human resource and diversity departments. It requires the active engagement of line management. Only by having holistic accountability of Latino retention can companies optimize their investment in Latino talent.

This chapter focused on proactive strategies that companies can follow to help improve the retention of Latino professionals. It also highlights best practices in several organizations who have been effective in keeping their top Latino performers. However, companies should not neglect the opportunity to analyze Latino retention effectiveness by studying Latino turnover. For example, if Latino employees tend to leave after only a short tenure with the company, this could signal problems in recruitment or in the socialization of new Latino employees. Losing a long-term Latino or a high-performing Latino professional may be the result of poor supervision or leadership.

Ultimately, effective retention requires organizations to place additional emphasis on determining the unique needs of their Latino employees. This is in sharp contrast to the retention strategies used by some employers that focus on imposing company and Anglo values on Latinos. Due to the growth of the Latino demographic and their significant presence in the U.S. workforce, there is a growing sentiment to permit Latino employees to define themselves and their employment needs in their own terms. Companies that are better able to allow Latinos to do this are in a much better position to address their needs as well as the business needs of the company (Ferdman and Davidson, 2002, p. 82). This approach supplies the formula that results in improved Latino employee retention.

CHAPTER 6

LATINO LEADERSHIP DEVELOPMENT

Changes in demographics and consumer markets make a focus on the development of Latino leaders not a luxury, but a necessity. Because our organizations are going to compete in a marketplace that is more diverse, organizations need leadership teams that represent that diversity. Organizations that fail to develop Latino leaders are at a disadvantage when it comes to their ability to meet current and future competitive demands.

Yet within organizations today, there is a resistance to Latino leadership development initiatives. Some managers erroneously believe that the Latino leadership development needs are no different than those of everyone else in the organization. Others think that their Latino employees would not want to be singled out by having leadership development programs created specifically for them. And there are still others who resist in the name of fairness with concerns that if they create a leadership development program for Latinos, they'll have to create one for every minority and underrepresented employee group in the company and they can't afford to do that.

The leadership development needs of Latino professionals are unique because their workplace experience differs from that of their coworkers. As discussed in Chapter 3, not only do certain cultural aspects tend to unite Latinos, these aspects also tend to make them different from non-Latinos. By creating initiatives specific to Latino development needs, organizations are able to address issues that otherwise would not be raised in traditional development initiatives.

Because Latinos tend to have different ways of viewing the world and the workplace, it is necessary to approach development differently. As discussed in Chapter 2, the L15 clearly indicates that the presence Latino talent is going to play a key role in a company's success. Because of this, companies faced with the choice of where to spend their training resources need to appreciate the business reasons for selecting Latino development initiatives.

If you believe that there is a need for strong Latino leaders, then the question becomes how best to develop them.

This chapter first looks at how Latino managers tend to have different experiences than their non-Latino colleagues. Based on these differences, this chapter suggests a recommended plan of action for companies looking to enhance the development of Latino professionals.

A MATTER OF DIFFERENCE

World-class leadership development programs often go to great lengths to ensure that their initiatives are tailored to the strategic initiatives and talent needs of an organization (Fulmer and Goldsmith, 2001). By taking this approach, companies can help their leaders develop a higher level of capability related to the core competencies of the organization. However, as our organizations become more diverse, it makes sense to consider the different experiences and paths that the leaders of our organizations have taken. An examination of these differences indicates that each leader possesses unique aspects that impact his or her leadership style. Developing new leaders requires consideration of these differences so that we can build on the unique experiences of our current leaders. To that point, this section sheds some light on how the Latino experience in the workplace may impact how organizations chose to develop the next generation of Latino leaders.

Overcoming Cultural Roadblocks

Because of their cultural script, some Latinos have to overcome ethnic roadblocks that may limit their ability to assume leadership positions. For example, placing the needs of family first may hinder job mobility and limit career advancement (Bean and Tienda, 1987; Elvira and Davila, 2005).

When job promotion opportunities arise, Latinos may not necessarily enter their names for consideration even if they have all the proper qualifications. Some Latinos might see the opportunity as posing too much risk because of the rejection they would experience if they are not selected. Latinos may perceive rejection as humiliation or disgrace. To avoid the possibility of being rejected, Latinos often choose not to apply for such opportunities (Sosa, 1999, p. 22). Because of this fear of rejection, Latinos will often wait and hope that they are approached with the opportunity.

For the most part, Latinos tend to accept their positions in the workplace because it provides a sense of stability. Ambition or attempting to obtain a promotion is not always admired in the Latino community. Those who aspire to higher positions may be labeled too competitive, too ambitious, or be seen as someone who is willing to attain his or her own goals at the expense of others. Such aggressive behavior can be perceived as leading to disruption in the workplace resulting in a loss of harmony and stability (Carr-Ruffino, 2003; Chong and Baez, 2005; Sosa, 1999).

Because of the cultural factors that discourage attainment of positions of higher responsibility, some Latinos prefer to play it safe and settle for positions that may not challenge their true capabilities, thus limiting their chances for greater success. Latinas may be especially susceptible to these cultural tendencies because some are taught to accept their place, resulting in less aggressive behavior and an inclination to wait patiently for things to improve (Chong and Baez, 2005, p. 82). Also, because successful Latino employees often excel in their ability to connect with members of their team or group, some might find it awkward if they are placed in a position of managing their peers. This could cause them to not apply for a group leader opportunity.

If an Anglo manager does not have adequate insight into the Latino culture, they may construe such behaviors as a sign of passivity or that the employee is not interested in moving up the ladder. They may mistakenly believe that the Latino employee is content staying where he is and that he lacks the conviction to aspire to greater things.

Cultural barriers also indicate how difficult it has been for those Latinos who have aspired to positions of leadership within an organization. Only 16 percent of the Latinos in the United States are in management or professional occupations. Organizations need to provide Latino employees with a variety of experiences that will broaden their perspectives, skills, flexibility, and overall effectiveness if this percentage is to increase.

Study of Latino Managers

In 1992, Dr. Bernardo Ferdman and Angelica Cortes published one of the few indepth studies of the experience of Latino managers working in an environment of mostly Anglo coworkers. The findings of this study, which was conducted in a medium-sized organization in the New England area, have helped American organizations better understand the experience of Latino managers for 15 years. But having a better understanding of the Latino manager experience also creates an obligation by organizations to use this insight to shape development programs that can help even more Latinos reach leadership positions. Because of the importance of this research, an overview of the findings of the study is provided in the following section and is highlighted in the sidebar Latino Experience in the Workplace.

Latinos have the pressure of dealing with the issue of cultural and ethnic identity in the workplace. This pressure is related to a

LATINO EXPERIENCE IN THE WORKPLACE

Latino managers have to deal with their ethnic and cultural identity at work. Ethnic identity relates to how strongly they identify themselves as being Latino. Cultural identity refers to their feelings of what being Latino represents.

Behaviors that come naturally for Latino managers are often misunderstood by their coworkers. Latinos thus are marked as being "different." This often leads to a feeling of isolation in the workplace.

Latino managers display behaviors that show their desire to "connect" with their coworkers and they expect these behaviors from their colleagues. However, most Anglo employees tend to prefer more distant work relationships.

Latino managers often sense resentment from colleagues after receiving promotions. This creates the burden of having to prove they are worthy of their roles.

Latinos feel that they have little in common with their coworkers. What is important to them are not the same things others consider important.

Source: Bernardo Ferdman and Angelica C. Cortes, "Culture and Identity among Hispanic Managers in an Anglo Business." In *Hispanics in the Workplace,* ed. S. Knouse, P. Rosenfeld, and A. Culbertson (Newbury Park, CA: Sage Publications, 1992): 246–277.

Latino's awareness of belonging to an ethnic group, together with the value and feelings that this membership evokes. This is pressure that most Anglo employees do not have to confront.

Also, Latino managers identified that behaviors that felt natural or appropriate to them had a tendency to be misunderstood by their Anglo coworkers. This resulted in Latino managers being marked as "different" because their behaviors were often in contrast with what was considered normal in the organization. Such an experience can cause Latino managers to feel isolated in the workplace.

The study also showed that Latino managers tended to treat others with respect and that they had a desire to form close connections with their coworkers and that they valued attending to the feelings of others. Because they saw these behaviors as advantageous in the workplace, they came to expect that they would be treated in the same manner. However, many of the Latino managers indicated that they did not receive the treatment that they were expecting. Their Anglo coworkers treated Latino managers as being competent and professional, but most did not choose to form close connections with them. Their Anglo counterparts tended to display leadership styles that were more distant and autocratic in nature.

According to the study, when some Latino managers received promotions, they reported sensing feelings of resentment by their Anglo coworkers. Thus, the Latino managers felt more of a burden to prove themselves than their Anglo counterparts who received promotions. They felt that their success on the job depended on their ability to become familiar with the prevalent norms of the organization. Anglo managers seemed to already possess this understanding.

Latino managers often felt that they had little in common with their coworkers. The things that other people considered important were not the same things the Latino managers felt were important. Latino managers developed a sense of community because of similar experiences they shared working in an environment of mostly Anglo coworkers.

While it is difficult to make broad generalizations based on the Ferdman and Cortes study, it does provide further evidence that Latino managers tend to be different from their non-Latino managerial colleagues. It is this difference that helps to justify the need to create leadership development programs catering to the unique needs and experiences of Latinos.

Latino Managers

Based on their experience in the workplace and their cultural script, Latino managers tend to lead in ways that differ from their Anglo counterparts. Some Latinos also view their role a bit differently. Because leadership development programs are designed to take managers to the next level of leadership, it is prudent to look at some Latino managerial tendencies.

Teamwork. Because Latino managers tend to focus on the needs of the group over the needs of an individual, Latino managers often place importance on instilling teamwork and a sense of group cohesiveness. It is common for Latino managers to have frequent group meetings with their employees and to have the group involved in decisions that impact the group.

Latino managers also have a tendency to share frequent updates on team progress and to celebrate team successes. Such efforts reinforce the Latino collectivist mindset. Also, Latino managers tend to establish rewards at the team level whenever possible as opposed to rewards based on individual performance. To help build trust within the team and trust in their ability to lead, Latino managers often promote a high degree of autonomy in their workgroups. By instilling a team mindset, Latinos managers reinforce their own sense of belonging.

Personal Relationships.   A Latinos' inclination toward *personalismo* does not end when they assume managerial positions. Latino managers tend to want to really get to know their employees. They may be more inclined to hold one-on-one discussions with their employees in an effort to get to know them better. Topics like an employee's family, their health, and their financial situation are often topics that Latino managers do not necessarily see as being off limits. Showing an interest in these areas often indicates their level of caring for the employee and does not present any legal issues as long as such personal information about an employee is not used in compensation or job opportunity decisions.

Non-Latino employees may be somewhat uncomfortable with a Latino manager's interest in their personal lives. What should be remembered is that such an interest is not intended to be intrusive, but is meant to establish a connection. Those higher up in the organization may also show some concern if they feel a Latino employee is getting "too close" with their direct reports. However, having a close relationship with their employees does not prevent them from being objective.

Giving Back.   Since Latinos are often uncomfortable with receiving individual acknowledgment for their accomplishments, they tend to credit their family and friends for their successes. Latinos often feel a sense of duty to give back and to support others. This tends to manifest itself by volunteering on committees, serving as an advisor or mentor, or helping those in need. The ability to give back and to help others is often a role that Latino managers relish.

Feedback.   Because Latinos form close relationships with their employees, they are likely to find the performance evaluation process a challenge. Latino managers may have a tendency to be concerned that giving employees constructive feedback may hurt their feelings or endanger the supervisor/employee relationship they have worked hard to nurture. Some Latinos may also want to take some accountability for an employee's shortcomings. Latinos may view an employee's deficiency as a sign of poor leadership on their part (Chong and Baez, 2005, p. 195). Similarly, Latino employees may view having to reduce the workforce as a reflection of their inability to lead effectively.

By looking at how some Latinos become managers, what experiences they have as managers, and what behaviors they demonstrate as managers, companies are better able to establish a framework on how to best meet Latino leadership development needs.

DEVELOPMENTAL NEEDS

Strategic leadership development programs involve more than just developing individual leaders. They focus on the context in which leadership is being developed. When dealing with Latino leadership development needs, the element of diversity must be added to focus on understanding, respecting, and valuing differences throughout the development process. In this section, we explore various leadership development methods and how their effectiveness may be influenced when taking Latino cultural differences into consideration.

360-Degree Assessments

Many organizations use 360-degree assessments as part of their leadership development process. This technique invites fellow employees to identify some of the leadership development needs of a Latino professional.

Often the results from such instruments have a significant impact on future leaders because the feedback tends to be clear, direct, and honest. Remarkable changes may occur when employees learn how their leadership style or behavioral tendencies impact others. Gaining a better understanding of how those above and below see managers often results in a higher sense of self-awareness (Rodriguez, 2005).

However, organizations need to be cautious about using such assessments to automatically identify developmental areas. The Latino cultural script may substantially influence the results. For example, Latinos tend to avoid conflict because of their desire to maintain harmonious relationships in the workplace. Other employees may interpret this behavior as a lack of assertiveness and passivity and thus mark the Latino employee low on this area.

So what should the organization do? Does it create a developmental plan instructing the Latino employee to be more assertive and to not shy away from conflict? Or does it view such results in an entirely different way? Clearly supervisors need to raise their level of understanding about Latino culture. But more importantly, it goes to the heart of the question whether an organization is going to define the needs of a Latino employee for them, or if it will allow Latino employees to define their needs based on their cultural lens.

Technology Solutions

More and more companies are leveraging technology to help tap into employee knowledge and expertise for leadership development purposes. Intranets and online communities of practice are technology-enabled methods used by organizations to help share both tacit and explicit knowledge held by employees. Organizations are realizing that all types of knowledge work require collaboration, experimentation, and shared experiences with other people who do similar work.

As Latinos progress through their careers, the types of changes they face will become more complex. Because of the sense of isolation some Latinos feel in the workplace, they may rely more heavily on their Latino peers not only for the sense of community, but to serve as a knowledge resource. If Latino employees are dispersed, maybe an online Latino community of practice could facilitate knowledge sharing among Latinos. Companies like Abbott Laboratories, the broad-based health care organization in Illinois, already taking the first steps toward Latino online communities (see the sidebar Corporate Best Practice—Abbott Laboratories.

CORPORATE BEST PRACTICE—ABBOTT LABORATORIES

Abbott Laboratories has established a web portal for their Latino employee network called LA VOICE. Latino employees use their web portal to exchange information, stay current on events, and to share documents. The portal provides a wonderful way for the dispersed members of LA VOICE to stay connected.

The online portal is used as a recruiting tool. The web site clearly identifies the vision and mission of LA VOICE and includes a quote from Abbott CEO Miles D. White showing his support for the organization. The web site also allows LA VOICE to articulate why Latino employees at Abbott should join the group, the benefits of membership and provides a registration link making it easy to join.

The web site also provides the structure of the organization and the names of the leaders of LA VOICE. Also provided is a listing and purpose of the various LA VOICE committees that members can join. The committees include Events, Community Relations, Recruitment, Personal/Professional Development, Cultural Awareness, Membership, and Communications. The committees allow LA VOICE members to get engaged in the activities in which they have an interest.

The web site also provides helpful resources. For example, a link to Abbott's Employee Referral Program is provided so that members may recommend the organization to friends and family. There are also links to several Latino professional organizations including

(continued)

the National Society for Hispanic MBAs, Hispanic Alliance for Career Enhancement, Society of Hispanic Professional Engineers, and the Association of Latino Professionals in Finance and Accounting. There are also links to Latino publications such as *Hispanic Business Magazine*.

The web site also provides a list of upcoming events that members can attend including a Breakfast Series with Latino Leaders, monthly lunch and learn events, and a mentoring fair. The web site also helps in member professional development by providing learning resources on a variety of topics including how to network strategically, how to conduct informational interviews, how to negotiate more effectively, and how to project more self-confidence.

LA VOICE is looking to add value in other ways. Soon a section that will share Latino success stories will be added as well as information on LA VOICE chapters. There will also be a quarterly newsletter that will highlight other aspects of LA VOICE and information about Abbott Latino business initiatives.

The interactive component of the web site already includes a message area where employees can submit comments.

While still in its infancy stage, the LA VOICE web portal already has the makings of a technology tool that can help members stay connected and it will soon be leveraged to further promote collaboration and professional development. Thus, the web site becomes a tool to help relieve feelings of isolation that some Latino employees may be feeling (especially those not located at Abbott's headquarters), while building a sense of community and serving as a knowledge resource.

What holds an internal Latino community of practice together is a real need for Latino employees to know what other Latino employees know. When high-potential Latinos are part of a community of practice, they can interact regularly and engage in joint activities that build relationship, trust, and collective knowledge with their Latino peers.

Companies looking for a model on how to leverage online communities for leadership development should benchmark IBM—one of the most successful firms in leveraging technology to help employees learn from one another. IBM relied heavily on technology when it rolled out a leadership development initiative called "The Role of the Manager," a companywide program designed to focus leaders on working with one another to identify and address pressing issues faced by their business units—and then to formulate action plans together with targeted strategies and goals.

This IBM leadership development initiative leverages technology through e-learning, management communities, and the full capabilities of the IBM intranet to help generate, capture, and share employee knowledge across the enterprise. For example, the program allows participants to work with their peers in virtual classrooms, e-labs, and collaborative sessions to build real-time awareness with live, online conferences and teaming.

Companies may want to consider doing the same thing for their Latino employees. For example, a company could role out a program called Latino Leadership and invite Latino employees to connect online to formulate plans on how companies can more effectively leverage aspects of Latino diversity or how an organization could better develop Latino professionals. The portal could also be used to gather Latino input on key leadership or business issues or allow top executives to dialogue online with Latino employees. It won't be too long before the integration of Latino leadership development programs and technology are the norm.

Mentoring

The inability to create and manage networks is a major barrier for nearly all nontraditional groups, including Latinos. These individuals often can't get the information they need about industry trends, unwritten business rules, and how to handle company politics adequately. That is why most people agree that mentoring is something high-potential employees need in order to succeed. Unfortunately, Latinos don't necessarily obtain these mentoring opportunities.

By pairing top Latino performers with internal senior executives, Latinos get exposure to new ways of thinking, knowledge, and perspectives, which help in their development. This leadership development method counts on senior executives to serve as role models, teaching their mentees how things work within the organization and how to get things done.

Mentoring also helps to expand a Latino's network within the organization by introducing him to decision makers and those with influence who can help him learn and grow. Providing a mentoring experience for high-potential Latinos is fundamental to the strategy of leveraging top executives to help hone the analytic abilities and instincts of the next generation of Latino leaders.

Knouse (1992, p. 138) points out six distinct benefits gained when a Latino employee is mentored. One is that the Latino mentee often gains some power based on the power of the mentor. Having a powerful mentor signals to others that the Latino employee should be taken seriously which increases the power of the mentee. Second, a mentor can put a Latino in situations and positions where he can demonstrate his competence. This often helps to reduce any negative stereotypes that some might have about Latinos. A third benefit is that mentors can provide coaching that often results in increased levels of self-confidence (Reich, 1986).

Latinos tend to have smaller but tighter social and professional networks (Vernon and Roberts, 1985). A mentor can help expand that network. Fifth, mentors act as role models and help a Latino learn the appropriate behaviors and values necessary to advance their careers (Gould, 1982). And finally, a mentor can help a Latino to acculturate faster.

But while most agree in the benefits of assigning a Latino professional a mentor as part of their development strategy, special considerations should be given to Latino mentee/mentor assignments. Probably the biggest consideration should be whether a high-potential Latino employee should have a Latino mentor or a non-Latino mentor. Both sides are explored here.

Non-Latino Mentor. Because there is a shortage of Latinos in positions of power within corporate America, it may be necessary for a Latino to have a non-Latino mentor. This has advantages and disadvantages. One advantage is that the Latino employee is likely to have a more powerful mentor if that mentor is in the majority group in the organization, such as an Anglo male. With power comes a larger network that the Latino employee can be exposed to (Knouse, 1992, p. 140). A non-Latino, especially an Anglo male, can better model the values and behaviors most common in the business world.

However, a non-Latino will probably not be able to identify with many of the aspects of what it means to be Latino. Having dissimilar values and behaviors may make it difficult for a strong connection to ensue. Closely related to a lack of identification is a potential lack of sensitivity to Latino issues. Lack of sensitivity could lead a non-Latino to discount the feelings of a Latino thus resulting in a perceived lack of support by the mentor (Korzenny and Schiff, 1987).

Latino Mentor. Having a Latino mentor usually results in greater rapport because both parties can identify with the Latino experience (Knouse, 1992). Sharing the Latino experience can also help the mentor recognize and empathize with the mentee and puts him or her in a better position to coach when there is a clash between cultures. Last, a Latino mentor serves as a role model regarding how to acculturate effectively. Having a Latino mentor might help to alleviate a feeling of isolation by a Latino employee.

But given that Latinos often are in positions of lesser influence, a Latino mentor tends to be less powerful than his Anglo counterparts. The few Latinos in positions that warrant them being considered to be a mentor usually receive many requests. Therefore, a Latino mentor may have less time to serve as a mentor (Ragins, 1989). Some companies take steps to eliminate this problem by identifying resources from outside the company. For example, General Mills hires external Latino executive coaches to help mentor and coach some of their Latino employees.

While the pros and cons of each situation should definitely be taken into account when making a Latino mentoring decision, so should other considerations. In a study by Blancero and DelCampo (2004), Latinos mentored by Anglos on averaged earned 17 percent more than Latinos mentored by Latinos. Gould (1982) also points out that the degree of acculturation of a Latino mentee should also be considered. For example, a first generation Latino would probably be best served by a Latino mentor because their high ethnic and cultural identity could pose a challenge for a non-Latino. Also, companies should always consider gender when making mentoring assignments. Gonzalez (1982) indicates that Anglo female mentors assigned to Latina mentees tended to be closest with regards to values while Anglo female mentors assigned to Latino male mentees tended to be the farthest apart.

Regardless of whether a Latino employee is matched with another Latino or a non-Latino, organizations should make sure to give proper attention to the unique development needs of Latino professionals. If Latino employees are mentored by non-Latinos, it is recommended that these non-Latinos receive some training to raise their awareness of Latino culture. In doing so companies will be better able to leverage a development process that has tremendous potential.

Also, some young Latino professionals may be hesitant to seek out mentors because they may be shy or not know how to approach someone to become a mentor. This restricts their opportunities for development. Organizations should help and encourage young Latinos to be proactive and to actively seek out mentoring relationships.

Action Learning

Organizations should consider putting Latino employees together to work on their company's key business issues and challenges through action-learning projects. Latinos can learn a great deal about strategy and business leadership in action-learning formats where they form teams to solve real business challenges faced by the organization.

These action-learning projects can give budding Latino leaders a firsthand taste of the leadership responsibilities to come. In addition to giving Latino employees a feel for the leadership functions they may one day serve, the program also helps establish working relationships with senior executives to whom they may report. In such programs, the required teamwork and the business challenge serve as the principle learning vehicles.

Organizations should consider migrating to this approach as a way to get high-potential, high-performing Latinos from middle management to the junior-officer level to expand their perspectives on how a business operates. Also, companies want more from investments in Latino leadership development efforts than just better-educated Latino executives. They want that education experience to benefit the company more directly. Because teams share their findings with senior executives, such programs permit Latino employees to serve as inhouse consultants to top management (see the sidebar Action Learning—Nightmare Scenarios).

Action Learning—Nightmare Scenarios

A possible action-learning project that could have immediate impact on a business is to have Latinos help an organization enhance its understanding of competitors in the Latino consumer market. This project could involve the creation of a new competitive analysis process. Latino leaders could be broken down into teams with each team assigned to study a major competitor in the Latino consumer market. The teams not only could analyze the competition's financials and capabilities, but can also be tasked with developing a behavioral profile of the competitors. This analysis could include a study of the culture, personality and management tendencies of the competition, along with their operational tactics.

Once each team has a more comprehensive understanding of the company's competition, they can be tasked with developing "nightmare scenarios" by outlining potential competitive tactics that could hinder the company's competitive standing in the Latino consumer market. Participants could then use these nightmare scenarios to develop strategies designed to improve their competitive position in the Latino market. These strategies can then be presented to senior management and if any of the recommendations are implemented, the result would be a stronger competitive position for the company in the Latino consumer marketplace. Of equal value is the holistic view of the competitive landscape gained by the Latino leaders—not to mention the development of their strategic thinking capabilities.

Source: Robert Rodriguez, "Involving Employees in Leadership Development," *Workforce Performance Solutions,* June 2005.

Action-learning projects also enhance the internal network of future Latino leaders. For many, this can be a key takeaway from such sessions because they have the opportunity to know more of their colleagues around the organization. They leave such an experience with the knowledge of who to call or where to go for answers or help executing their plans. This is critically important because success in business has so much to do with building and sustaining relationships.

Executive-Led Learning

Organizations should also consider asking current Latino executives to facilitate leadership development sessions and workshops for Latino employees. These organizations realize that leadership lessons are best learned from those who are trusted and well respected inside their own organizations and within the Latino community. Also, using executives as teachers facilitates the socialization of more junior leaders because it provides exposure to decision making and the leadership style used by current Latino leaders.

Executive-led learning brings credibility to the development process because the audience listens firsthand to the ideas, points of view, and issues facing current Latino executives. They realize that good companies don't just teach their managers and leaders—they learn from them. Some organizations like PepsiCo and Wachovia customized nondegree Latino leadership development courses with business schools like UCLA and Kaplan University where company executives facilitate and share lecture duties with Latino faculty professors.

Such programs allow participants to hear firsthand, and unfiltered, the key messages about business goals and strategy from their Latino executives. Latino executives bring the frame of reference and keen insights that future leaders appreciate and value. Such sessions also provide Latino executives with the opportunity to model the leadership behavior and perspective they desire in future leaders. For the Latino employees, it also makes the executive a bit more approachable.

When top Latino executives are involved, future Latino leaders gain a realistic understanding of the leadership behavior that is expected of them and a deeper understanding of business strategy.

The key to supporting executive-led sessions is to have Latino leaders personalize the content of the strategy sessions. When preparing to lead their respective sessions, Latino leaders can tap into the "teachable moment" philosophy of author and business school professor Noel Tichy (1998). This also allows Latino executives to realize that not only do they have a point of view about how the company operates and how to get things done, but they also have to invest the time and effort to make those points of view "teachable" to other Latinos. The best Latino role models help Latinos learn how to think on their own rather than telling them what to think.

Online communities, 360-degree assessments, mentoring, action-learning projects and executive-led learning all have one thing in common: They focus on the social aspect of organizational life that plays into the Latino cultural script. In order for these efforts to be successful in advancing the development of Latino employees, they need to be supported by an organizational culture that promotes the sharing of knowledge and collaboration.

Organizations that have an overly competitive culture, where a "survival of the fittest" mentality exists, will have difficulty implementing Latino leadership development programs that rely on employee involvement. In such environments, the hoarding of knowledge is seen as a way to guarantee success and thus limits the effectiveness of such programs. Major problems can occur if companies ignore the people and cultural issues. Having employees help in the development of the next generation of Latino leaders leads to success. In an environment where an individual's knowledge is valued and rewarded, establishing a culture that recognizes tacit knowledge and encourages employees to share it is critical. The need to sell this concept to employees shouldn't be underestimated.

In many cases, employees are being asked to share their knowledge and experience—the very traits that make them valuable as individuals—with their Latino coworkers.

Latinos who are part of leadership development programs often find themselves under continuous scrutiny. These newly appointed Latino leaders face one of the most challenging periods of their professional lives as they try to understand the environment, set directions, and prove their worth. Once in place, many find themselves lonely, time-poor, and facing a plethora of issues with constantly shifting priorities—all within the political climate at the top of the organization and with the added potential of feeling isolated.

It is important to realize that such Latino leadership development efforts help to champion the new values that are at the heart of a knowledge-based enterprise. Some experts are calling this the "principle of fair exchange," when Latino employees believe that they are being treated fairly for the intelligence, creativity, innovation, experience, and passion they bring to their work and share with coworkers.

Because these future leaders typically accept the burden of translating ideas into action, Latinos can benefit from a common and clearer understanding of the knowledge relationship they have with their coworkers. Future leaders need to realize that such efforts help to build common language, methods, and models around specific competencies that are important to an organization. By including Latinos, they also embed knowledge and expertise into a larger percentage of the employee population. This helps increase Latino access to expertise across the company and takes advantage of an organization's most valuable asset—the collective expertise of its employees.

Companies are embracing a new equation for success: Knowledge equals power, so share it and it will multiply. This new logic represents a radical rethinking of basic business and economic models and is a driving force behind the increasing involvement of employees in Latino leadership development efforts (Rodriguez, 2005).

DEVELOPMENT WITH A LATINO PERSPECTIVE

Organizations spend a lot of time and money creating comprehensive leadership development programs. Usually a key component of such efforts includes a desire to have such programs immediately improve company performance. To do this, such programs are aligned with the culture of the organization and with core business strategies.

Large corporations usually have a centralized group handle leadership development for the entire organization; however, the development of management and business skills is handled by business units (Fulmer and Goldsmith, 2001). At the corporate level, leadership development focuses on core issues related to effective leadership such as values, strategic change, and ethics. World-class leadership development programs connect work experience with other development methods to enhance business knowledge and to create a better understanding of the whole organization.

For these reasons, high-potential Latinos should be included in centralized leadership development programs. However, what is becoming evident is that Latinos also need development programs that look at leadership issues from a Latino point-of-view. Leadership development programs designed specifically for Latinos also permit them to leverage their unique capabilities and use their "Latino-ness" as an asset. Such sessions also allow Latinos to celebrate their ethnic heritage. Simultaneously, such programs allow Latinos to confront the challenges posed by being seen as "different" from everyone else. The following items are worthy of consideration when developing leadership development programs designed specifically for Latino employees.

Latino Only

Such sessions should include only Latino employees and, whenever possible, be facilitated only by Latino executives and Latino external faculty or facilitators. This helps to create a "safe" environment that allows participants to openly share their thoughts, ideas, and experiences. If Latinos do not feel that the environment is safe, they are less likely to open up and this reduces the learning. When there are non-Latinos present, Latinos may spend time and energy explaining and defending their point of view. This leaves less time and energy to focus on development.

Having Latino facilitators and faculty will also help in the design of the program because they will be more inclined to appreciate the Latino cultural nuances that need to be incorporated. Also, Latino participants are more inclined to listen to and respect the messages delivered by those who are "just like them." Latino facilitators and faculty also allow for greater reciprocal interactions, which helps to create an optimal learning experience.

This will be the first experience for many of the participants to take part in a leadership development program exclusively with other Latinos. This will likely be a memorable and often unique occasion when they do not have to deal with being "different" from everyone else.

Time for Networking

Given that Latinos are inclined to want to form relationships with others, plenty of time for networking among participants should be incorporated into the design of such a program. As participants get to know each other, a sense of community and inclusion emerges. This further advances the possibility that members will openly share their experiences and increases the probability that they will support each other.

More importantly, networking allows Latino professionals to form a group of their peers that they can count on for advice, support, or help even after the development session ends. The ability to tap into a network of Latino professionals who share the same experiences will likely be invaluable to the participants. To allow sufficient time for such networking and community building, programs should run over multiple days.

Program Content

Once these elements are taken into consideration, the focus can now move into the content of a Latino leadership development program. The content of these programs should consist of traditional development topics as leadership, change management, team building, and related topics. However, these topics should be explored from a Latino point of view. For example, how does cultural heritage impact a Latino's leadership style? How does the Latino cultural script impact performance in teams? The following elements should be included.

Latino History and Contributions. Many Latinos do not know much about their culture and its rich history. Latino leadership development programs should include an overview of Latino history in the United States. A discussion about the many rich contributions that Latinos have made should also be included. Such topics provide a foundation and thus should be covered early on in such programs. A review of Latino contributions helps to instill a sense of pride in Latino culture among the participants. The Latino Leadership Institute at UCLA begins with a session that covers Latino history from the settlement of St. Augustine, Florida, in 1565 up to the current debates over immigration occurring today.

Latino Identity.   Much has been written in this book about the struggles that many Latinos have with their cultural and ethnic identity. The fears of being stereotyped or typecast are real for Latino professionals and many spend considerable time dealing with the negative images of Latinos that tend to be common among Anglo coworkers (Ferdman and Cortes, 1992, p. 268). Latino professionals struggle with how to best maintain their individuality without losing their Latino identity.

For these reasons, it is highly recommended that every Latino leadership development program address the topic of identity as a key component of the curriculum. Since Latino identity is a complex topic, organizations should consider seeking the counsel of Latino or diversity experts in designing exercises aimed at helping Latinos deal with the issue of identity in the workplace. Discussions on identity can also address the issue of acculturation, assimilation, whether being seen as a Latino delegitimizes their accomplishments in the eyes of others, and whether emphasizing their Latino-ness creates divisiveness in the workplace. The online Latino leadership development courses at Kaplan University, for example, spend considerable time helping Latino participants look at the issue of cultural and ethnic diversity. Participants are guided through techniques that help them become more comfortable with how they view themselves. Attendees are provided with strategies that allow them to deal more effectively with how others view them thus reducing their probability of feeling isolated in the workplace.

Corporate Culture.   Corporate culture defines the proper way to think, act, and behave within an organization (Schein, 2004). Organizational leaders define what is considered proper within an organization through their actions and behaviors, by how they allocate resources, and through the things they reward and punish.

Those who do things in the proper way tend to fit in, survive, and ultimately become successful.

Having a thorough understanding of corporate culture is essential for Latinos for two reasons. First, as they progress in their careers, they will be placed in positions that have an impact on shaping the culture of a department, business unit, or the entire organization. Knowing how to establish a healthy culture, or how to change an unhealthy one, will serve them well as leaders as they look to align culture with the business strategy of the organization. Second, being knowledgeable about culture can also help Latinos better understand why they sometimes feel like they do not fit in. This knowledge better prepares Latinos to leverage the values and principles associated with diversity and inclusive work environments to not only help them adapt, but to more effectively integrate their cultural heritage into the workplace. This not only helps Latinos succeed, it helps the organization take advantage of the diversity that Latino employees bring. Understanding culture also helps Latinos with acculturation.

Assessment.   Research suggests that the better people understand themselves, the better enabled they are to develop effective strategies to interact with others and respond appropriately to the demands of their work environment. Latinos will thus benefit from having a better understanding of their own communication patterns, behavioral tendencies, and motivators. Having a strong sense of self also allows Latinos to leverage the uniqueness they bring to the workplace and results in a greater probability that they will be able to maximize their performance.

As part of Latino leadership development programs, organizations should include the use of self-assessment tools such as Myers-Briggs or other assessment instruments. By knowing more about themselves, Latino employees can develop action plans that will help them grow both personally and interpersonally. People project who they are to the outside world in a certain manner. However, Latinos may lack the awareness of the effect their cultural script has on others. For example, Latinos may believe that they are acting in very respectful ways when they exhibit *simpatía*. However, to a non-Latino, the behaviors that support *simpatía* may be construed by non-Latinos to mean Latinos are subservient (Sosa, 1999, p. 9).

Increased self-awareness of their management style can also help a Latino be a better leader. By being comfortable with their uniqueness, Latino managers are better able to value the uniqueness that others bring to the workplace. This can be especially helpful if Latino managers lead teams that include many non-Latinos.

Conflict Management. Conflict is a normal, inevitable element within organizations. How employees deal with conflict determines whether conflict helps or hinders the organization. This holds especially true for Latinos who have a natural tendency to avoid conflict in order to maintain simpatía (Marín and Marín, 1991). Organizations should consider including discussions on the topic of conflict management as part of their Latino development programs with the goal of allowing Latino employees to see conflict from a broader perspective and to convey that conflict does not necessarily contribute a lack of harmony.

Since Latinos tend to have a predisposition to avoid conflict, they benefit from training that provides them with alternative strategies on how to respond to conflict. Avoiding or yielding to conflict every time it occurs may not always be the best approach in maintaining relationships and may hinder the overall performance of the group. But as highlighted earlier, such training should not be about changing them (Latinos) to be more like the rest of the organization. Rather, training can help Latinos use *simpatía* as a strength in conflict resolution. Conflict provides an opportunity for collaboration that places value on the nature of the relationship. This approach allows Latinos to embrace their cultural script while simultaneously enhancing their performance.

Cross-Cultural Communication.   Latino leaders would also benefit from a discussion of cross-cultural communication. Some Latinos may be unaware of their communication styles and may assume that others communicate in the same way—what has been referred to as "projected similarity" (Cruz, 2001). Problems can arise when Latinos interpret the communication of non-Latinos through their own cultural lens. This false assumption of similarity could result in miscommunication or misunderstanding between Latinos and their non-Latino colleagues.

For example, Latinos tend to get close to the person with whom they are speaking. This might violate a non-Latino's "personal space," causing the person addressed to back away. Latinos might interpret this backing away as being standoffish or showing prejudice. Similarly, Latinos tend to be more comfortable with physical contact when communicating with others and are more inclined to touch the person they are addressing. For non-Latinos, such touches in a work setting may be uncomfortable. A Latino may misinterpret this and assume their non-Latino colleagues are being rude.

Communication by its very nature is interactive. Sessions that help Latinos with their cross-cultural communication abilities can help them better foster cooperation, as opposed to animosity, with their non-Latino colleagues.

SUMMARY

Research (Gallegos and Ferdman, 2007; House, 1983) shows that Latinos flourish in work environments when they are supported in four areas: (1) emotional support that meets their empathy, kindness, love, and trust needs; (2) instrumental support that helps them do their jobs more effectively; (3) informational support to deal with personal and professional problems; and (4) appraisal support that is relevant for self-examination and cultural comparison. Latino leadership development programs meet Latino needs in all four of these support areas.

Leadership development programs geared specifically for Latinos also helps them in three fundamental ways. First, it allows Latinos to focus on the conceptual foundation of leadership. With this foundation, they are better able to analyze the similarities and differences in the leadership styles of Latinos and non-Latinos. Second, by letting Latinos examine their behavioral and cultural tendencies, it lets them identify potential barriers to their success. Finally, such programs provide time to work on practical leadership development needs in a safe environment, which ultimately enhances their leadership abilities.

More importantly, such leadership development programs acknowledge that Latinos are indeed a powerful force in the U.S. society and labor force. These workshops allow Latinos to have a voice in their development needs by removing them from the dominant group perspective and providing a Latino point of view. This not only raises their sense of pride in their cultural heritage, it better prepares them to harness their heritage for the benefit of the organization. In short, it allows them to be their authentic self.

A Latino leadership development program helps Latinos who feel isolated tap into their community for strength and rejuvenation. Latinos are thus connected to a peer group who can provide support and guidance on how to navigate the political agendas and other roadblocks in the workplace. In exchange for providing an opportunity to dialog about their heritage and by investing in their developmental needs, Latinos will develop a heightened sense of loyalty resulting in increased retention and commitment.

As Latinos play an increasing role in the success of U.S. businesses, efforts that develop their capabilities will become ever more important. By implementing some of the development strategies identified in this chapter, organizations better prepare Latinos to make significant contributions at the individual, managerial, and organizational level.

CHAPTER 7

SHAPING THE FUTURE

How many of the top 10 U.S. industrial companies from 100 years ago can you name? Names like the Pullman Company, Central Leather, American Sugar, U.S. Steel, and American Tobacco come to mind. Somehow, these companies failed to anticipate and adjust to the future, and it ultimately led to their inability to remain on top.

One possible reason for their failure could be that they paid insufficient attention to external signals that were providing warnings of future changes. Another reason could be that they remained trapped in yesterday's business models. Yet another reason could be simple corporate arrogance and hubris. Regardless of the reason, things may have turned out differently for these firms had they paid more attention to the external cues that were signaling upcoming changes in the marketplace and labor force demographics (Schoemaker, 2002).

Imagine that your company could go back in time 10 years. Now ask yourself what things your company missed out on through the past decade that could have impacted their present success. What were those external signals that—had your firm noticed and reacted to them—would have put the company in a better competitive position in the marketplace? Unfortunately, companies cannot actually go back 10 years. But your organization can begin preparing itself to look for external signals that might help make it more successful 10 years from now.

This book has painted a picture of the future by looking at the nature and impact Latinos will have on society and on the workforce. The Latino 15 outlined in Chapter 2 should provide significant signals about some future changes that are fast approaching due to the growing U.S. Latino community. The insight provided will help companies craft a number of talent management strategies to better prepare themselves for the future where Latinos will play an increasingly important role.

As a result of reading this book, you have the chance to identify potential strengths and opportunities for improvement related to Latino talent management initiatives, or lack thereof. Many of these might otherwise go unnoticed by leaders focused obsessively on the organization's present day talent mix. Organizational leaders need to make strategic decisions related to their Latino talent management initiatives today that will be sound for various future scenarios. By doing so, they put themselves in a position where they are better prepared to deal with their future.

Human resource executives, diversity practitioners, and business unit leaders can play a valuable role in helping to ensure the success of their organizations by better leveraging their Latino talent (Rodriguez, 2006c). This forward-looking approach allows organizations to devote resources toward projecting new core competencies to better develop and manage the Latino presence in the labor force. Latinos within the organization can contribute to new product development, new industry alliances, and help an organization tap into the Latino consumer market in many other ways.

If organizations want to play an active role in helping to shape the future of Latinos in the workplace, they should consider placing additional emphasis on Latino educational attainment, research that focuses on Latinos, and Latino workplace integration. By focusing on these areas, companies can help to ensure that the pipeline of future Latino talent remains strong and steady.

LATINO EDUCATIONAL ATTAINMENT

The Achilles' heal of the Latino community is educational attainment. As mentioned in Chapter 2, less than 60 percent of Latinos in the United States finish high school. If you look at Latinos of Mexican descent, who represent approximately two-thirds of the Latino population in the United States, the statistics are even more discouraging: slightly more than 50 percent finish high school and less than 8 percent have an undergraduate college degree. For the U.S. economy, this should serve as a warning sign regarding our ability to remain competitive in the global market place. As the Latino population continues to grow in the United States, more needs to be done to drive higher levels of educational attainment.

High School

In order to identify potential solutions to low educational attainment, it is prudent to look at some of the root causes. According to a study by the Pew Hispanic Center (Fry, 2005), Latino students are much more likely than Anglo or African American students to attend high schools that are public, very large, have many students on federal subsidies, and have higher teacher-to-student ratios. For example, 56 percent of Latinos attend large (more than 1,800 students) public high schools versus only 26 percent of Anglo students.

According to the National Center for Educational Statistics (NCES), these characteristics matter because they tend to have a significant impact on student performance (2005). Lower student achievement and higher drop out rates are more prevalent in schools with a large enrollment (Fry, 2005). Lower school performance is also associated with those schools having high student-to-teacher ratios as well as those with higher concentrations of low socioeconomic status students. By attending schools that are underfunded and underperforming, Latinos do not receive adequate preparation for college courses.

Another factor contributing to the low level of educational attainment in the Latino community is the high dropout rate for Latinos who were born outside of the United States. Nearly 25 percent of all school dropouts were born outside of the United States. Many of the recent Latino arrivals to this country were already behind in school before they left for the United States (Fry, 2005).

The relatively high teenage pregnancy rate for Latinas also contributes to the dropout rate. According to the National Campaign to Prevent Teen Pregnancy, over half (51 percent) of Latinas become pregnant before the age of 20, compared to only 35 percent of all adolescent girls (Deconto, 2006). Teenage pregnancy increases the odds that Latinas will drop out of high school to take care of the child or to obtain work to help pay for child-related expenses.

College

An undergraduate degree is widely accepted as a fundamental educational goal. Employers often help to set this expectation by offering substantial financial rewards to those who complete their undergraduate degree.

According to the National Center for Education Statistics, those who have an undergraduate degree earn approximately 67 percent more annually than those without an undergraduate degree. Unfortunately, Latinos lag every other population group in earning a college degree (Fry, 2002).

The U.S. Census indicates that approximately 12 percent of Latinos have an undergraduate degree. This does not compare favorably to the approximately 30 percent of the Anglo population that has an undergraduate degree. There are several explanations for the lower level of college educational attainment. First, approximately 40 percent of Latinos who complete their high school degrees enroll in community colleges. Few who complete their two-year associate degree go on to complete a bachelor's degree.

Second, many of the Latinos who enroll in four-year college programs are in schools that are less selective and have lower college graduation rates (Fry, 2004). Of Latino students enrolled in college, only 57 percent complete their degrees compared to 81 percent of Anglo students who successfully complete their degrees.

A third contributing factor to the low level of college educational attainment for the Latino community is that many are pursuing their degrees on a part-time status—25 percent of Latino students are enrolled part-time versus 15 percent for Anglo students. Attending school on a part-time basis generally means students are working while going to school. The demands of part-time work and part-time school decrease the odds of their successfully completing their degree.

The Latino cultural aversion to loans and debt are also contributing factors to poor college graduation rates. Many Latinos equate not having to obtain loans to a strong work ethic. Thus, young Latinos are taught that if you can't pay for things in cash, then you need to work for it as opposed to getting into debt. This philosophy encourages Latino students to not attend unless they can pay in cash.

According to the National Center for Education Statistics, Latinos borrow the least of all undergraduates by race or ethnicity. One of the reasons Latinos are reluctant to take out loans is because they do not want to put themselves in a position where they are repaying a college loan even if they are not successful in completing the degree.

Without taking out loans for college, Latinos have to use a pay-as-you-go method and if cash runs out, they have to stop their studies. This often prolongs their study programs, increasing the risks of never finishing the degree. Additionally, this approach to college funding often means that Latino students are not as well prepared for their courses due to limited study time resulting from a heavy work schedule (Vara-Orta, 2007).

Last, Latinos are more likely to delay or prolong their college education into their mid-20s and beyond. For example, a higher percentage of students who are over the age of 24 enrolled in college courses are Latinos (Fry, 2002). Delaying or prolonging college education often decreases the likelihood of graduation.

Solutions

The cumulative impact of these high school and college factors create huge obstacles for Latinos to overcome on their quest for advanced educational attainment. However, organizations cannot afford to stand by without taking a more active role in helping to increase the educational levels of Latinos. Global competition and an increased demand for knowledge workers means that employers are being forced to take a more active role in enhancing the level of education by Latinos. A failure to improve Latino educational attainment will severely hinder an organizations ability to meet their business objectives due to shortages in highly educated, highly skilled employees. There are some areas that warrant future exploration by organizations who are looking to take a proactive role in raising Latino education levels.

Many of the parents of today's Latino and high school students did not attend college. Because Latino parents have no personal experience with higher education, it is difficult for them to orient, support, and counsel their children. Therefore, young Latinos receive almost no information about the college experience from their parents (Hughes, 2003). Since many young Latinos are the first in their families to pursue a college degree, they lack the guidance and support from their parents that many Anglo college students take for granted.

Corporations should consider sponsoring parent education programs. Such programs could cover a variety of topics including 529 college savings plans, sources for scholarship, and student preparation techniques for college entrance exams such as the ACT and SAT. Organizations can also help to demystify the college entrance process by reviewing topics such as advance placement courses, strategies for selecting a college, and key submission dates for college and financial aid materials.

But beyond covering technical and procedural topics, such programs should also address cultural issues. For example, the topic of college education funding should be explored. As mentioned earlier, Latino cultural beliefs may interfere with obtaining loans for education. By discussing loans in a manner that outlines the tradeoffs or implications such an approach entails, this belief can be modified. Other cultural elements include the desire for Latino parents to have their children attend college closer to home, even if they have opportunities to attend more prestigious colleges farther away.

Because Latinos often lack role models with college educations or professional positions, some parents may not be able to envision their children in top schools or in professional positions. This topic could be addressed so that Latino parents see all that is possible for their children. Such programs should be facilitated by Latino community leaders whenever possible. This takes advantage of the *respeto* aspect of the Latino cultural script.

Hewitt Associates, described in Chapter 4, established and funded a career center in a predominantly Latino high school, raising the awareness of career choices and college possibilities. Such career centers reduce student truancy and high school dropout rates. Companies could also send some of their Latino professionals to high schools and colleges to discuss various career options or to share their personal success stories. Hearing from successful Latino professionals helps raise the awareness of career possibilities and provides role models for young Latino students.

Companies can provide college internship opportunities specifically for Latino students. Many organizations have established corporate work study programs with high schools to help students raise money for future college tuition providing them with valuable corporate world experience and exposing them to new career possibilities (see the sidebar Cristo Rey Corporate Work Study Program).

CRISTO REY CORPORATE WORK STUDY PROGRAM

Cristo Rey Jesuit High School offers a Catholic college preparatory education for the immigrant families of Chicago's southwest side. Established in 1996, Cristo Rey has 225 students who come from the predominantly Latino communities of Pilsen and Little Village, Chicago neighborhoods whose population is 88 percent Latino.

In order to make private, college-preparatory education affordable, Cristo Rey developed an innovative work-study program for high school students called the Corporate Internship Program (CIP), which combines two commonly used business concepts, employee leasing and job sharing. This initiative gives the students a means of financing their education. CIP allows each of their students to earn 65 percent of the cost of their education by working five full days each month in entry-level positions at corporations in downtown Chicago. Over 90 companies participate in the CIP—Chicago's major banks, law firms, hospitals, and consulting firms such as McKinsey, JP Morgan Chase, Aon, Ernst & Young, Leo Burnett Worldwide Advertising, and many others.

Each sponsor company is assigned a team of four Cristo Rey students. These students rotate through a Monday thru Friday work schedule sharing one job. The students perform standard office clerical and mail clerical work in the corporate offices of the sponsor company. Sponsoring companies pay approximately $30,000 annually for each job-sharing team of four students.

The results of this innovative program have been tremendous: 97 percent of the students participating in the program have received ratings of "Outstanding" by their sponsor companies. The program was initially designed to pay the costs of running the school for students who otherwise would not have the financial opportunity to attend a private, college preparatory school. However, there are many other benefits to the students. The program has evolved into an innovative means of providing students with crucial hands-on, white-collar work experience, while simultaneously empowering them to take an active part in financing a major portion of their education. As a result of working in a business environment, students acquire desirable job experience and marketable skills, develop a network of business contacts, gain exposure to a wide variety of career opportunities, refine a strong work ethic, and increase their self-esteem.

Sponsor companies gain the benefit of knowing they are helping to fill the pipeline with talented Latinos. To learn more about the Cristo Rey corporate work study program, go to www.cristorey.net.

The statistics related to the level of educational attainment of Latinos clearly indicate that things need to change in order to have a better prepared, highly educated workforce in the future. If companies fail to take steps to fix this issue, they increase the probability of a future where a significant portion of the U.S. population does not have the adequate skills and education required to compete in a global environment.

LATINO WORKPLACE RESEARCH

According to Ferdman and Cortes, "Much of the research about Latino cultural features is based on investigations of Latinos in the context of largely Latino organizations, primarily in Latin America. There is a danger of directly applying group-level findings abroad to minority experiences in the United States. Prior accounts derived from group-level analysis of people in their native cultures do not allow us to predict readily individual behavior in the context of minority roles" (1992, p. 266).

This conveys a need for organizations and academic institutions to partner to learn more about the Latino work experience in the United States. A survey conducted by the Pew Hispanic Center (2002) showed that 8 out of 10 Latinos feel that they are victims of discrimination in the workplace. If this survey result accurately reflects how the majority of Latinos feel, then organizations have much to learn about how to best support Latino employees in the workplace and how various talent management programs impact Latino professionals. For example, what is the impact on workplace productivity and level of engagement of Latino employees who are struggling with their sense of identity in the workplace?

A review of the academic literature shows study after study on issues related to education, public policy, demographics, and so on. We need more research, however, on the impact of Latino talent management initiatives like the ones described in this book. There is broad consensus in research circles that companies are not doing a good job of meeting the needs of Latino employees and that a significant percent of our labor pool is not being fully utilized. But unfortunately, companies have few resources, and even less guidance, on how best to connect with their Latino employee population.

Without more sound research on the subject of Latino talent management programs, human resource executives, diversity practitioners, and business leaders run the risk of being criticized-for being ill informed in their adoption of particular workplace practices with regard to Latino employees (Johnson and Duberley, 2000).

Research on Latino talent management issues generates knowledge that organizations can apply to improve the Latino experience in the workplace. What is needed is a greater partnership between academia and practitioners to determine the most effective Latino talent management practices. In such a partnership, academics can help with diagnosis, while practitioners can focus on the application. If done well, the research can help everyone better understand what drives success when it comes to Latino talent management practices.

One area that warrants more study involves trying to identify what workplace conditions best support Latino employees? Such research findings can have a tremendous impact on encouraging more effective management in a work environment that has an increasingly Latino identity.

What do Latino employees really want? More insight into this area could help with identifying intrinsic and extrinsic rewards or motivators. What helps to enhance Latino employee self-confidence? The list of potential research questions is endless.

Another consideration regarding research is the manner in which we conduct our research or data gathering. Much of the research today takes a more negative approach, that is, organizations study what is "broke" and then try to fix it based on what has been learned. For example, many organizations conduct exit interviews of high-potential Latino employees to try to identify the reason they are leaving. Such an approach focuses on problem analysis.

Instead of taking this negative approach, we can obtain richer information by asking current Latino employees questions such as, "During your time with our organization, what has been your

SAMPLE LATINO EMPLOYEE APPRECIATIVE INQUIRY QUESTIONS

1. Describe the most energizing moment in your professional life. What made that experience possible?
2. Describe your peak mentoring experience. What made that interaction so rewarding and special?
3. Describe a time when you have felt most recognized and acknowledged for what you contribute to this organization.
4. Describe the best on-the-job experience you've had working on a project with someone of the opposite sex.
5. Think of someone at work who you admire and who says things that resonate in you. What is it about this person that you admire?
6. Think back in your adult life and think of a person for whom you have a great deal of trust and respect but didn't always agree with. When you disagreed with this person, how did you communicate that? What made it possible for you to respect that person?
7. Describe a time when you were a part of a team that had a high level of trust and respect among the team members. How was trust and respect displayed? What made it possible to establish trust in the group?

high point, a moment when you felt really effective and engaged? Describe how you felt and what made that situation possible?" Some refer to this approach as "appreciative inquiry" which basically looks at peak moments to see what elements consistently are mentioned. Organizations could benefit greatly by conducting appreciative inquiry questions of their Latino employees to better understand those moments when the employee has felt most alive, excited, and truly engaged within the workplace. A sample listing of appreciative inquiry questions companies can ask their Latino employees appears in the sidebar Sample Latino Employee Appreciative Inquiry Questions. Such information could help practitioners better create the work environments of the future that would allow Latinos to experience such peak moments more often.

Another way to study Latino talent management initiatives is to create an event where Latinos from both inside and outside of an organization can come together to share ideas, best practices, engage in dialogue, and formulate strategies. Such a gathering can provide a powerful demonstration of a company's commitment to their Latino employees and customers. You can also provide workshops, hold panel discussions, and include Latino motivational speakers. This could also provide a wonderful opportunity to connect Latinos with their peers to help form friendships, enhance their network of Latino peers, and possibly identify potential mentor/mentee partnerships.

Conducting more research and providing opportunities for Latinos to highlight their peak moments and to share their best practices are wonderful ways to generate knowledge about the Latino experience today in order to create Latino talent management programs that will be valuable to both the organization and Latino employees in the future.

A VISION OF THE FUTURE

Picking up on clues and signals related to Latinos and conducting more research about the Latino experience will definitely provide practitioners with information they can leverage to create effective Latino talent management practices for the future.

A clear vision on how a company will address Latino talent management issues in the future provides a clear and compelling catalyst for change. The more vibrant and engaging description that a company can create about the future, the more meaningful it will be for organizational leaders and the more inspirational it will be for Latinos.

The ability to manage the continuity and change related to Latino talent management practices will depend on having this vision of the future clearly in mind (Collins and Porras, 1996). The acronym LATINO is offered as a potential starting point for organizations to shape their positive guiding image of the future.

(L)isten

Marginal voices often go unspoken if their discourse is unacceptable. Latinos sometimes suppress their opinions because they do not believe anyone will listen. Organizations should strive to emancipate all of the silenced Latino voices and ensure that no Latino voice goes unheard. If Latinos feel that their voices are not solicited or listened to, they will voice their displeasure by leaving the organization.

(A)cculturation

Organizations should strive to create a work environment where Latino employees do not feel that they have to assimilate in order to fit in. Allowing Latinos to acculturate provides them an opportunity to bring their whole self to work. By embracing their Latino heritage, they will simultaneously adopt some aspects of American culture. When Latinos are allowed to acculturate, they are better able to exchange cultural elements and meaning with non-Latinos.

(T)alk

Organizations should strive to include an ever-increasing number of Latino voices in the conversations about Latino talent management practices. By expanding the circle of dialogue, companies will be better able to tap into the hopes, strengths, assets, and dreams of their Latino employees. Also, talking with Latino employees more often provides the space for them to make their contributions more apparent. So sit back, talk with Latinos, and enjoy the interchange.

(I)nquiry

Organizations should master the art of inquiry by enhancing their ability to ask powerful questions. Have a common practice of starting constructive conversations with Latino employees by engaging them in inquiry. The practice of inquiry is vital because it helps draw out Latino stories, dreams, and wishes that typically remain unexpressed. Having their voice solicited through inquiry allows Latinos to experience renewed levels of growth, increases self-confidence, and provides new opportunities for collaboration. A sense of curiosity by non-Latinos ultimately results in a signal of affirmation.

(N)urture

Companies should continually strive to identify the conditions that nurture equality in the workplace. By doing so, organizations ensure that no one voice dominates another. If Latinos are made to feel inferior in comparison to others, subtle but pervasive hierarchies are established. Nurturing equality enhances the development of a sense of community, promotes the exploration of new knowledge, and leads to the acceptance of the wide array of diverse experiences that Latinos bring. Nurturing an environment that promotes equality also raises the possibility of taking advantage of Latino diversity.

(O)bserve

Companies should observe and celebrate the differences that Latinos bring to the workplace. When differences are not observed or celebrated, people will tend to attack when confronted with a differing point of view. Usually these attacks come in the form of criticism and results in Latinos having to take an aggressive stance in order to defend their uniqueness. Organizations should strive to create an environment where Latino differences are observed, embraced, and not ignored.

SUMMARY

In a book designed to explore Latino culture and its impact on talent management strategies, making generalizations about Latinos is inevitable. The intent of this book is not to promote overly broad generalizations or stereotypes, but to offer insight into the enormous variations that exist in the Latino culture and how those variations unite Latinos while at the same time distinguishing them from non-Latinos.

The United States has successfully integrated immigrants into the fabric of its society for over two centuries. In doing so, Americans have been influenced by and have embraced various aspects of the cultures of others. As more and more Latinos join the labor force, their cultural script will influence and impact the workplace. If organizations embrace some of these cultural elements, as opposed to imposing non-Latino values on them, they will better meet the needs of their Latino employees (Ferdman and Gallegos, 2001).

There is no one single answer to how companies can more effectively attract, retain, and develop Latino professionals. However, the strategies provided in this book provide a starting point for the journey many more companies will begin to take on their way to creating environments where Latino employees are allowed to maximize their potential and performance to help raise not only their level of job satisfaction, but also the financial success of the organization.

This book serves not as an end but as a beginning to a healthier organizational life for Latinos. It is an invitation to look at organizational life in another way, not as the only truth. Consider this an invitation to deliberate about the workplace of the future.

CHAPTER 8

FROM ONE LATINO TO ANOTHER

I decided to write this final chapter in the first person as a way to share my voice. As I began writing this book, it occurred to me that there would be many Latinos who would read this book. I quickly realized that this provided a wonderful opportunity for me to connect with my fellow Latinos. It provided me a chance to develop my own sense of *personalismo* with my audience. With this opportunity, I decided to share some personal advice with my Latino readers. These "words of wisdom" have been shaped by my own experience and have helped me reach a certain level of success. It is my sincere hope that by sharing my story and passing along some insightful tips, some of you will be better prepared to follow your dreams.

Before I begin, it might be good if you knew more about me. I was born in Lubbock, Texas, to parents who were migrant workers. My father was born in Matamoros, Mexico, and immigrated to the United States at a young age. He followed all the necessary immigration procedures and officially became a naturalized U.S. citizen when he was in his 20s. My mother was born in Brownsville, Texas, the daughter of a Mexican father and Spanish mother.

I recall my parents making trips to work the cherry fields in Michigan and the sugar beet fields in North Dakota as migrant workers. My father quickly realized that the life of a migrant family made it difficult to focus on the educational needs for me and my two younger brothers. We eventually settled into the Latino community on the west side of St. Paul, Minnesota. We grew up with modest means and my parents continuously reminded me that the secret to a richer life was an education.

I received good grades in high school but when it came time to decide on whether to go to college, I found myself quite lost. It seemed like all of my Anglo friends knew what to do regarding getting into college. Since no one in my extended family had gone to college, I was left to figure out the college application process on my own. I eventually decided to attend a state university. The main reason I chose the school, however, was because that was where most of my Anglo friends had decided to go. I figured if the university was good enough for them, it was good enough for me. Later I found out that I had been accepted to some much better schools but I didn't know much about what it meant at the time to go to a top-tier university.

College was an enjoyable experience. Fortunately, I met a professor who helped me understand my career options. He encouraged me to join the Inroads organization and soon I was doing summer internships in the field of human resources with Target Corporation, my sponsor company. The internships exposed me to Corporate America and I became excited about the possibility of working in such an environment after graduation. I joined 3M Company after receiving my bachelor's degree and I began my career as a human resource professional.

After several successful years at 3M, I felt it was time to obtain my master's degree. 3M's tuition reimbursement program and flexible work environment allowed me to finish my graduate degree. While I learned a great deal and was able to perform at a much higher level as a result of my graduate school experience, I was left struggling with one part of my learning experience. I realized that throughout my undergraduate and graduate school work, I never had a Latino or Latina professor.

This bothered me greatly and I shared my frustration with one of the mentors I had at the time. What my mentor told me changed my life. He asked me why, if I was so upset with the lack of Latino professors, wasn't I doing anything about it? His comment put me back on my heels. Was he suggesting that I should become a professor? As I thought about his comment more and more, I realized he was right. I soon enrolled in a doctoral program designed for adult working professionals. I was only 28 at the time I enrolled and was the youngest doctoral student in my program.

I earned my PhD and started on a career as an academic, initially teaching in the MBA program at DePaul University in Chicago. DePaul has a relatively high Latino student population and I could see the look of appreciation from the Latino students in my class. Like me, many had not previously had a Latino professor. It felt good to have some of them share that they saw me as a role model. Some of them have indicated that they too are now considering pursuing their doctorate degree.

There is one more thing I'd like to share before proceeding to offer advice. As a Latino professional myself, there have been times in my career when I have struggled to feel fully included and understood in my work environment. When I tried to understand why I felt this way, it occurred to me that quite often my approach to work contrasted with that of my mostly Anglo coworkers. This led me to feel pressured to modify my approach to work so that I could be more accepted by my colleagues. However, the new behaviors I was demonstrating did not feel natural to me. I felt like I was not behaving or speaking with an authentic voice and, at times, I knew it was impacting my performance in a negative way.

After many years of reflection, I was finally able to grasp why I felt this way. I realized that in order to feel included in the workplace, I often had to deny aspects of myself that were part of my Latino heritage. After having this realization, I decided to more fully embrace my Latino culture. What has happened since has been quite remarkable. Ever since I embraced my own "Latino-ness," I have been able to perform at a much higher level and have been able to make greater contributions in my personal and professional life. My colleagues have also noticed that I convey a higher degree of self-confidence. I became aware that my Latino heritage is an asset and, by embracing it, I was being my true self.

My own experience has been the inspiration that led me to write this book. I shared my story with a friend of mine, Raymond Arroyo, chief diversity officer at Aetna. He indicated he had had the same experience. He said that for the first 15 years of his career, he was somewhat neutral about his Latino heritage. It was buried inside of him. However, he too felt something was lacking. When he began to embrace his Latino heritage, he felt "liberated and redis-covered." By embracing his whole self, he felt more powerful and empowered. I could relate to how Raymond felt. I figured there may very well be many other Latinos out there who are feeling like Raymond and I felt—misunderstood and possibly ignored.

Now that you have more information about my own back-ground and my journey so far, I offer you these 10 tips.

TEN TIPS

Tip 1: Commit to Lifelong Learning

Given that I have a PhD, it is probably not a big surprise that I'm a big proponent of lifelong learning. Lifelong learning definitely includes finishing high school and earning advanced degrees. As a community, we will struggle to be taken seriously if we do not improve our level of educational attainment. Individually, earning a degree often exposes us to a whole new way of viewing the world. A college degree also helps us "learn how to learn." By becoming more proficient at analyzing information and gleaning insights from data and situations, we become much more knowledgeable about ourselves and the world around us.

I realize that earning an undergraduate or graduate degree is not possible for everyone. Not being able to earn a degree does not mean you must stop learning. No matter what degree you have earned, maintain your passion for more knowledge. Focus on not only learning more about the world around you, but also on learning more about yourself as an individual. For example, I keep on learning by reading vigorously—a book, magazines, reports. I am always reading something.

Part of lifelong learning also involves an ability to periodically sit back and reflect on your past accomplishments. Study what has worked for you and what hasn't and learn from your past. Also, if you have a passion for learning so will your children. Set an example, be a role model—continue learning.

Tip 2: Leverage Your Strengths

I'm a big believer that our greatest room for growth is not in trying to fix our weaknesses, but in more fully identifying and leveraging our strengths. Most of us remain inefficient in leveraging our strengths. I recommend that you find the time to identify those things that you are truly good at. The fastest way to maximize your performance in the workplace is to focus on your strengths, not try to fix your weaknesses. Work usually provides us with many opportunities to get ahead. But if we are to take advantage of these chances when they arise, we need to understand where we are strong, develop these areas to their fullest potential, and then find a position that allows us to leverage our strengths.

I recommend the book, *Now, Discover Your Strengths,* written by Buckingham and Clifton (2001), consultants at the Gallup

Organization. It provides some wonderful insights into the concepts of strengths, talents, and weaknesses. This book also allows you to access an online survey that helps you identify your strengths. I took the survey about five years ago. One of the strengths it identified for me was that I excel on projects that are seen as being significant and highly visible. The tool helped me to realize that I enjoyed opportunities where I could stand out, be seen as significant in the eyes of others, and be appreciated for my unique contributions.

After discovering this strength, I looked for opportunities to leverage it. In academia, one way to be recognized is to publish articles. I quickly learned that I had a knack for writing articles that could get published. In the past five years, I've published over 25 articles in a variety of magazines and journals. Also, I spoke at numerous conferences and seminars. This too allowed for a certain amount of visibility not only for myself, but for my organization. Kaplan University has placed me in positions where I can use these strengths. By focusing on developing these strengths, as opposed to trying to focus on a weakness, I have been able to perform at a high level—I have put myself in a position where I can do what I do best every day.

A focus on our strengths does not need to be limited to our work capabilities. It can also relate to our Latino cultural heritage. We also need to be clear about what things give us strength and then we need to protect them. Another friend of mine, Rosie Saez, director of the Leadership Practices Group at Wachovia, shared with me how being close to her family gave her strength. Early in her career, she had an opportunity for a promotion that would require her to relocate. Even though she wanted the job, she knew that because of her family situation she could not relocate. She knew she had to make some tough choices and set some boundaries. She told Wachovia she couldn't take the job because of her family. Fortunately, Wachovia provided her with a flexible work arrangement so she could still take advantage of the promotion opportunity while remaining close to her family. She has performed wonderfully ever since and is one of the highest ranking Latinas at Wachovia—all because she focused on the things that gave her strength.

Tip 3: Learn about Latino History and Culture

Latinos have a rich and long history and we have contributed much to society. As our Latino population continues to grow, we will have increased visibility as a community. Having a stronger understanding about our heritage and culture will instill in us a renewed sense of pride. Unfortunately, many professional Latinos lack a good understanding of Latino history and I believe it somewhat limits our success. We are not able to own our own power unless we can relate to and understand what Latinos have accomplished, and suffered, in the past.

By history, I don't just mean memorizing names and dates, I mean looking at the cause and effect of things related to our Latino community. Understand the how's and why's related to our culture. My own knowledge about Latino history is somewhat limited. But as I learn more about who we are as Latinos, it helps me better understand why we sometimes do the things we do or why we look at the world in a certain way. Our contributions are possible because we stand on the shoulders of the Latinos who came before us. Knowing more about the contributions they have made allows us to show appreciation for their role in helping to shape our community.

Also, be comfortable in inviting non-Latinos to look at your culture. Be open to people when they ask questions about your culture. Your coworkers may be exhibiting a genuine interest in your culture so don't assume they intend to be offensive.

Tip 4: Deliver Results

None of us ever wants to feel that we were given certain things simply because of our ethnicity. Sure we want our ethnicity to be valued and appreciated, but we want to be rewarded based on how we have performed in our roles. When it comes to work and earning recognition, there is no substitute for delivering results and performing at a high level.

Unfortunately, there will be those who believe that successful Latinos are only in their positions because of Affirmative Action or because our companies needed "to fill a quota." The only way to combat those who look to minimize our success is to demonstrate, through sustained levels of high performance, that we have earned the positions that we are in. Delivering more than people expect of you over and over again will give you an impressive reputation and will gain you credibility and influence in the workplace.

Tip 5: Be Bilingual

The ability to speak Spanish is only going to increase in importance as our Latino community continues to grow. Speaking Spanish will help us to effectively communicate with a greater number of people. It also provides a wonderful way for us to stay connected to our ethnic heritage. My own Spanish isn't as strong as it should be. Growing up in Minnesota, I didn't have too many Spanish-speaking friends. At home, our parents spoke to us in Spanish, but as I grew older, I began to speak to them only in English. And like with most languages, if you don't use it, you lose it. While I can understand Spanish, I'm still working on enhancing my Spanish-speaking capabilities. I look with envy at my Latino colleagues who can speak Spanish fluently. I also encourage you to teach your children Spanish, they will thank you for it in the future. Their Spanish-speaking ability will be an asset and will provide them with an advantage in the workplace.

Tip 6: Network

I highly encourage you get out and meet others in your profession, whether they be Latino or not. Having a strong network will often result in rather surprising benefits. A strong network gets you access to an even greater number of people who you can turn to for help, advice, or information. More importantly, it puts you in a position where you can help others in your network. This ability will strengthen your relationships.

However, be sincere when you network. Some people only begin to network when they are looking for a job. If you approach people to network only when you need something, they will feel you are trying to use them. Also, when others network with you, don't do it because you expect them to pay you back. Do it because you want to build a relationship. If you make a promise to someone in your network, keep it. Chances are they know others in your network as well and you don't want them to share with others that you don't keep your word.

Tip 7: Give Back to Your Community

Those who have achieved certain levels of success have hardly done it alone. Because of this, they have an obligation to give back to others. When we give back, we strengthen our communities and we help to develop the next generation of Latino leaders. Giving back can include mentoring a Latino student, serving on a board of directors for a Latino nonprofit organization, or volunteering at a Latino-related educational event. Especially for Latinos, our communities are a big part of who we are. By giving back, we help our community grow. The area that probably needs our greatest help is education. Find ways to support and improve others' educational experience. Even if you give back only a little bit of your time, you will enjoy a great deal of satisfaction. If you don't give back, you run the risk of losing your connection with the Latino community.

Tip 8: Vote

In order for Latinos to be represented adequately in our local, state, and national government, we have to exercise our right to vote. If we fail to vote, we run the great risk of having others decide for us. Don't think that your vote doesn't matter. There have been many elections over the past few years where winners have been determined by a hundred votes or less. Whether our excuse is apathy or just sheer laziness, voting has become a privilege that many in our community have taken for granted. Whether it be in your local, state, or federal elections, make your voice count and vote. Do not risk becoming an invisible community.

Tip 9: Choose your Employer with Care

As I have mentioned in this book, there is currently a greater demand for top Latino talent than there is supply. Because of this, some of you will be in positions to be very selective about where you work. Don't take the selection of your next employer lightly. Ask questions about their Latino talent management initiatives. Ask to speak with current Latino professionals in the organization. See what Latino organizations they support.

The employment contract between an employer and an employee has changed over the past dozen years or so. The days of an employee working their entire career for only one organization are gone. As organizations struggle to meet Wall Street expectations and to compete on a global scale, downsizings and restructurings are increasingly causing more and more employees to seek new job opportunities. Also, the stigma of being a "job hopper" has been reduced as employees realize they are not obligated to stay with employers who do not treat them well or where they are not actively engaged. The Bureau of Labor Statistics indicates that the average length of tenure for employees with one company is only about four years. So in reality, the question becomes not "if" you will leave your current employer, but "when."

Since the days of "lifetime employment" are all but gone, the new paradigm is that of employees seeking "lifetime employability." Lifetime employability involves selecting employers who will enhance your skills and capabilities and allow you to gain new experiences. Being exposed to such work situations makes you more "employable" in the long run. Your marketability is thus enhanced should you find yourself needing to seek another employer.

Employers have realized this change in the employment relationship as well. What they have come to realize, however, is that the more they invest in an employee's skill and capabilities (thus making them more marketable), the more likely an employee is to stay. It is almost counterintuitive. Groom someone to leave and they are more likely to stay.

Tip 10: Become Financially Savvy

Some of us come from countries with poor financial institutions and unstable economies. Because of this, we are leery of banks and other financial institutions. It is not uncommon to hear about *abuela's* stockpile of cash hidden in the bed mattress. What I recommend is that you explore ways to handle your money more wisely. Find ways to make the money you have work for you. Things like 401k plans, investments, and IRAs are all ways we can get the most out of our financial resources.

As discussed in Chapter 3, many of us focus on the present and not as much on the future. This tendency is one that I do not wish to criticize. However, we should realize that this tendency to ignore the future may hurt us financially in the long run. I encourage you to seek the advice of a certified financial planner or accountant to help you make the most of your financial situation. Being smarter with our money helps enhance our financial security that in turn provides us with more peace of mind and, ultimately, more choices.

Summary

My hope is that you found these tips helpful. Even though they may be somewhat simplistic in nature, that does not mean they are not powerful. Some of these tips will resonate with you, others won't. That's Okay. Embrace the tips that you found most useful and incorporate them into your daily life.

APPENDIX

LATINO ORGANIZATIONS AND PUBLICATIONS

ORGANIZATIONS

American Association of Hispanics in Higher Education (AAHHE). AAHHE is a cross-disciplinary, higher education organization primarily focused on the need to develop Latino faculty and senior administrators as well as serving as a leading research and advocacy group for Hispanic higher education issues. www.aahhe.org

ASPIRA Association, Inc. ASPIRA is the only national non-profit organization devoted solely to the education and leadership development of Puerto Rican and other Latino youth. www.aspira.org

Association for the Advancement of Mexican Americans (AAMA). AAMA is committed to advancing the lives of at-risk and disadvantaged youth and families through an array of innovative programs of excellence in the areas of education, health and human services, and community development. www.aamainc.com

Association of Hispanic Entrepreneurs (AHEUSA). AHEUSA promotes the business development of Hispanic entrepreneurs with economic programs designed to strengthen and expand the income potential of its members and affiliates in the trade area; educating the business community and representing the association in city, county, state and national legislative and political affairs; expand the association into any regions where significant number of Hispanic entrepreneurs can be found. www .aheusa.com

Association of Latino Professionals in Finance and Accounting (ALPFA). ALPFA is the leading professional association dedicated to enhancing opportunities for Latinos in the accounting, finance and related professions. ALPFA is a not-for-profit entity registered with the Internal Revenue Service. Membership is open to anyone who shares our values, mission, and principles. www.alpfa.org

Association of Mexican American Educators (AMAE). AMAE strives to ensure equal access to a quality education at all levels for the Mexican American/Latino students where cultural and linguistic diversity is recognized and respected. www.amae.org

Congressional Hispanic Caucus Institute (CHCI). A non-profit and nonpartisan educational organization established in 1978, CHCI's mission is the development of the next generation of Latino leadership actively involved in the American policy-making process. CHCI's vision is an educated and civically active Hispanic community participating at the local, state, and federal policy decision-making levels. www.chci.org

Congressional Hispanic Leadership Institute (CHLI). CHLI seeks to provide charitable and educational assistance to and advance the diversity of social and cultural thought among the millions of Americans of Hispanic and Portuguese descent. www.chli.org

Council of Latino Agencies (CLA). CLA's mission is to support and promote its members for the betterment of the community, and act as a voice of the Latino community in the District of Columbia. www.consejo.org

Cuban American National Council (CNC). CNC is a nonprofit organization headquartered in Miami, Florida, with offices in Washington, DC; Central Florida; and Union City, New Jersey. CNC provides human services to persons in need from all racial and ethnic groups, assists individuals to become self reliant, and builds bridges among America's diverse communities. www.cnc.org

Hispanic Alliance for Career Enhancement (HACE). HACE is a national nonprofit organization dedicated to incubating and nurturing Latino careers through career development programs for Latinos in high school, college, and in the early stages of their careers. HACE also provides programs to connect professional Latinos with leading institutional, government, and corporate employers. www.hace-usa.org

Hispanic American Center for Economic Research (HACER). HACER's goal is to promote the study of issues pertinent to Latino countries as well as Hispanic Americans living in the United States, especially as they relate to the values of personal and economic liberty, limited government under the rule of law, and individual responsibility. HACER does this by both generating and supporting independent research. www.hacer.org

Hispanic Association of Colleges and Universities (HACU). HACU's mission is to champion Hispanic success in higher education. Their fast-growing membership of 450 colleges and universities, including 50 international members, are leaders in educational innovation and effectiveness; they serve nearly three of every four of the more than 2 million Hispanic college students in the United States. www.hacu.net

Hispanic Association on Corporate Responsibility (HACR). Founded in 1986, HACR is one of the most influential advocacy organizations representing 14 national Hispanic organizations in the United States and Puerto Rico. Their mission is to advance the inclusion of Hispanics in corporate America at a level commensurate with Hispanic economic contributions. www.hacr.org

Hispanic National Bar Association (HNBA). HNBA is an incorporated, nonprofit, national association representing the interests of over 33,000 U.S. Hispanic attorneys, judges, law professors, legal professionals, legal assistants or paralegals, and law students. HNBA's mission is to improve the study, practice, and administration of justice for all by ensuring the meaningful participation of U.S. Hispanics in the legal profession. www.hnba.com

Hispanic Business Women Alliance (HBWA). HBWA is an on-line community of Hispanic women entrepreneurs, professionals, consultants, executives, inventors, and investors located throughout North America, Latin America, the Caribbean, and Spain interested in doing business and collaborating with each other. www.hbwa.net

Hispanic Educational Telecommunications System (HETS). HETS is the first bilingual distance learning consortium dedicated to serving the higher education needs of the fast-growing Hispanic communities. Founded in 1993, HETS's membership is comprised of 15 colleges and universities in the mainland United States, Puerto Rico, and Latin America. www.hets.org

Hispanic Scholarship Fund Institute (HSFI). HSFI was created in 2001 to extend the impact of the Hispanic Scholarship Fund (HSF) on the achievement of Latinos in the United

States. Working with HSF on the goal of doubling the rate of Hispanic college graduates by the year 2010, the primary focus of HSFI is to engage the public sector in support of Latino higher educational achievement. www.hsfi.org

Hispanics in Philanthropy Association (HIP). Founded in 1983 to promote stronger partnerships between organized philanthropy and Latino communities, HIP has developed into a transnational network of grant makers committed to strengthening Latino communities across the Americas. www.hiponline.org

Institute for Latino Policy. A privately-funded nonprofit and nonpartisan policy center focusing on issues of concern to Puerto Ricans and other Latinos in the New York area. www.latinpolicy.org

Julian Samora Research Institute. An organization committed to the generation, transmission, and application of knowledge to serve the needs of Latino communities in the Midwest. To this end, it has organized a number of publication initiatives to facilitate the timely dissemination of current research and information relevant to Latinos. www.jsri.msu.edu

Latin Business Association. Established in 1976 as a private nonprofit organization, the Latin Business Association delivers innovative programs and services that enhance the success and growth of Latino entrepreneurs. www.lbausa.com

League of United Latin American Citizens (LULAC). LULAC's mission is to advance the economic condition, educational attainment, political influence, health, and civil rights of the U.S. Hispanic population through community-based programs operating at more than 700 LULAC councils nationwide. www.lulac.org

Mexicans and Americans Thinking Together (MATT). MATT is a nonprofit organization whose mission is to encourage bicultural Mexicans and Americans to understand, address, and solve the major problems of our two nations to the benefit of both peoples. www.matt.org

National Association of Hispanic Journalist (NAHJ). NAHJ is dedicated to the recognition and professional advancement of Hispanics in the news industry. Established in April 1984, NAHJ created a national voice and unified vision for all Hispanic journalists. www.nahj.org

National Association of Hispanic Publications (NAHP). NAHP is a not-for-profit trade agency representing leading Hispanic publications in 41 markets and 39 states with a combined circulation of over 14 million. Membership includes newspapers and magazines, which reach over 50 percent of the Hispanic households in the United States. www.nahp.org

National Association of Latino Elected Officials (NALEO). A nonpartisan membership organization whose constituency includes the nation's more than 6,000 elected and appointed Latino officials. www.naleo.org

National Association of Latino Fraternal Organizations (NALFO). NALFO's purpose is to promote and foster positive interfraternal relations, communication, and development of all Latino fraternal organizations through mutual respect, leadership, honesty, professionalism, and education. Established in 1998, NALFO has 23 member organizations in the United States. www.nalfo.org

National Council of La Raza (NCLR). NCLR is the largest national U.S. Hispanic civil rights and advocacy organization. NCLR conducts applied research, policy analysis, and advocacy, providing a Latino perspective in five key areas: assets/investment, civil rights/immigration, education, employment and economic status, and health. www.nclr.org

National Hispanic Corporate Council (NHCC). NHCC is a nonprofit organization whose purpose is to provide its member corporations with the resources, market intelligence, collective expertise, education, and counsel to implement proven strategies for reaching the Hispanic community externally and leveraging Hispanic talent internally. www.nhcc-hq.org

National Hispanic Employee Association (NHEA). NHEA a national network of Hispanic employee associations that promotes career development through education, mentoring, and networking activities to advance the social and economic status of the U.S Hispanic community. www.mentores.org

National Society for Hispanic Professionals (NSHP). NSHP is the leading Hispanic nonprofit 501©(6) professional networking association for Hispanic professionals in the United States and the Americas. It currently has over 10,000 members and growing. www.nshp.org

National Latina Organization (MANA). MANA is a nonprofit, advocacy organization established in 1974. Its mission is to empower Latinas through leadership development, community service, and advocacy. www.hermana.org

National Puerto Rican Coalition (NPRC). NPRC's mission is to systematically strengthen and enhance the social, political, and economic well being of Puerto Ricans throughout the United States and in Puerto Rico with a special focus on the most vulnerable. www.bateylink.org

National Network of Latin American Medical Students (NNLAMS). In 1987, regional Latino medical student groups formed NNLAMS, an organization comprised of five regions representing active Latino students in the U.S. medical schools. www.nnlams.com

National Society of Hispanic MBAs (NSHMBA). NSH-MBA fosters Hispanic leadership through graduate management education and professional development. NSHMBA works to prepare Hispanics for leadership positions throughout the United States, so that they can provide the cultural awareness and sensitivity vital in the management of the nation's diverse workforce. www.nshmba.org

National Society of Hispanic Professionals (NSHP). The mission of the National Society for Hispanic Professionals is to empower Hispanic professionals with information and connections. NSHP's purpose is to provide Hispanic professionals with networking and leadership opportunities and information on education, careers, and entrepreneurship. www.nshp.org

New American Alliance Institute (NAA). NAA's mission is to become the premier organization promoting strategic philanthropy in the Latino community and leveraging the significant resources of large charitable organizations to make a greater contribution to the Latino community. www.naaonline.org

Puerto Ricans in Management and Executive Roles (PRIMER). PRIMER is a network of business and professional leaders who leverage resources to create opportunities, sponsorship, and success for its members and that of Puerto Ricans/Latinos in the United States. The network enables its members to grow to their full potential and fulfill critical mentorship and leadership roles. www.primernetwork.org

Society of Hispanic Professional Engineers (SHPE). SHPE is a leading social-technical organization whose primary function is to enhance and achieve the potential of Hispanics in engineering, math, and science. www.shpe.org

Society of Mexican American Engineers and Scientists (MAES). MAES promotes excellence in engineering, science, and mathematics while cultivating the value of Latino cultural diversity. www.maes-natl.org

United States Hispanic Chamber of Commerce (USHCC). Through its network of more than 150 local Hispanic Chambers of Commerce and Hispanic business organizations, the USHCC effectively communicates the needs and potential of Hispanic enterprise to the public and private sector. www.ushcc.com

BUSINESS PUBLICATIONS

Hispanic Business Magazine: www.hispanicbusiness.com

Hispanic Magazine: www.hispaniconline.com

Hispanic Network Magazine: www.hnmagazine.com

Hispanic Today: www.hispanic-today.com

Latino Leaders Magazine: www.latinoleaders.com

PODER Magazine: www.poderforum.com

REFERENCES

Alcalay, R., F. Sabogal, and J. R. Gribble. 1992. Profiles of Latino health and implications for health education. *International Quarterly of Community Health Education* 12, no. 2: 151–162.

Badillo, H. 2006. *One nation, one standard.* New York: Penguin Group.

Bean, F. D., and M. Tienda, 1987. *The Hispanic population in the United States.* New York: Russell Sage.

Berry, J. W. 1980. Acculturation as varieties of adaptation. In *Acculturation: Theory, models and some new findings,* ed. A. M. Padilla, 9–25. Boulder, CO: Westview.

Blancero, D., and R. G. DelCampo. 2004. Hispanics in corporate America. *Hispanic MBA Magazine,* December.

Buckingham, M., and D. Clifton. 2001. *Now, discover your strengths.* New York: Free Press.

Buckingham, M., and C. Coffman. 1999. *First, break all the rules.* New York: Simon & Schuster.

Carr-Ruffino, N. 2003. *Managing diversity: People skills for a multicultural workplace* (6th ed). Boston, MA: Pearson Custom Publishing.

Center for Women's Research. 2000. *Latina entrepreneurs: An economic force in the U.S.* Washington, DC: Center for Women's Research.

Chong, N., and F. Baez. 2005. *Latino culture: A dynamic force in the changing American workplace.* Yarmouth, ME: Intercultural Press.

Collins, J., and J. Porras. 1996. Building your company's vision. *Harvard Business Review* 74, no. 5: 65–77.

Cruz, W. 2001. Differences in non-verbal communication styles: The Latino-Anglo perspective. *Leadership and Management in Engineering* 1, no. 4: 51–53.

Deconto, J. J. 2006. Hispanic teenage pregnancy rate is high. *News and Observer,* November 11.

Deforest, M. E. 1994. Hispanic staffers: Management and motivation. *Long Term Care Management* 43, no. 3: 43.

Diaz-Saenz, H. R., and P. D. Witherspoon. 2000. Psychological contracts in Mexico. In *Psychological contracts in employment: Cross-national perspectives,* ed. D. M. Rousseau and R. Shalk, 158–175. Thousand Oaks, CA: Sage.

D'Iribarne, P. 2002. Motivating workers in emerging countries: Universal tools and local adaptations. *Journal of Organizational Behavior* 23, 1–14.

Domino, G. 1992. Acculturation of Hispanics. In *Hispanics in the workplace,* ed. S. Knouse, P. Rosenfeld, and A. Culbertson, 56–74. Newbury Park, CA: Sage Publications.

Domino, G., and A. Acosta. (1987). The relation of acculturation and values in Mexican-Americans. *Hispanic Journal of Behavioral Sciences,* 9, 131–150.

Elvira, M. M., and A. Davila. 2005. *Managing human resources in Latin America: An agenda for international leaders.* New York: Routledge.

Espinosa, G., V. Elizondo, and J. Miranda. (2003). *Hispanic churches in American public life: Summary of findings.* Notre Dame: IN, University of Notre Dame Institute for Latino Studies.

Ferdman, B., and A. C. Cortes. 1992. Culture and identity among Hispanic managers in an Anglo business. In *Hispanics in the workplace,* ed. S. Knouse, P. Rosenfeld, and A. Culbertson, 246–277. Newbury Park, CA: Sage Publications.

Ferdman, B., and M. N. Davidson. 2002. A matter of difference and inclusion: What can I and my organization do about it? *Industrial-Organizational Psychologist* 39, no. 4: 80–85.

Ferdman, B., and P. I. Gallegos. 2001. Racial identity development and Latinos in the United States. In *New perspectives on racial identity and development: A theoretical and practical anthology,* ed. C. Wijeyesinghe and B. W. Jackson III, 32–66. New York: New York University Press.

Figueredo, D. H. 2002. *The complete idiot's guide to Latino history and culture.* New York: Penguin Group.

Flynn, G. 1994. HR in Mexico: What you need to know. *Personnel Journal* 73, no. 7: 34–42.

Fry, R. 2002. *Latinos in higher education: Many enroll, too few graduate.* Washington, DC: Pew Hispanic Center.

Fry, R. 2004. *Latino youth finishing college: The role of selective pathways.* Washington, DC: Pew Hispanic.

Fry, R. 2005. *The high schools Hispanics attend: Size and other key characteristics.* Washington, DC: Pew Hispanic Center.

Fulmer, R. M., and M. Goldsmith. 2001. *The leadership investment: How the world's best organizations gain an advantage through leadership development.* New York: American Management Association.

Gallegos, P. V., and B. Ferdman. 2007. Identity orientations of Latinos in the United States: Implications for leaders and organizations. *Business Journal of Hispanic Research* 1, no. 1.

Gonzalez, A. 1982. Sex roles of traditional Mexican family: A comparison of Chicano and Anglo students' attitudes. *Journal of Cross-Cultural Psychology* 13, 330–339.

Gould, S. 1982. Correlates of career progression among Mexican-American college graduates. *Journal of Vocational Behavior* 20, 93–110.

Grow, B., R. Grover, A. Weintraub, C. Palmeri, M. Der Hovanesian, and M. Eidam. 2004. To tap the Hispanic market, you first have to understand it. *BusinessWeek,* March 15.

HispanTelligence Report. 2006. U.S. Hispanic media market: Projections to 2010. *Hispanic Business,* April 19.

Hofstede, G. 1980. *Culture's consequences: International differences in work-related values.* Beverly Hills, CA: Sage.

House, J. S. 1983. *Work stress and social support.* Reading, MA: Addison-Wesley.

Hughes, A. T. 2003. *Building Latino diversity.* Chicago: Hispanic Alliance for Career Enhancement.

Humphreys, J. M. 2006. *The multicultural economy 2006.* Athens, GA: University of Georgia, Terry College of Business, Selig Center for Economic Growth.

Johnson, P., and J. Duberley. 2000. *Understanding management research.* London: Sage Publications.

Kikoski, J. F., and C. C. Kikoski. 1999. *Reflexive communication in the culturally diverse workplace.* Westport, CT: Quorum Books, Praeger Publishers.

Klein, S. A. (2007). Beyond sombreros: The right way and wrong way to sell products. *Crain's Chicago Business,* March 5.

Knouse, S. B. 1992. The mentoring process for Hispanics. In *Hispanics in the workplace,* ed. S. Knouse, P. Rosenfeld, and A. Culbertson, 137–150. Newbury Park, CA: Sage Publications.

Kochhar, R. 2006. *Latino labor report: 2006: Strong gains in employment.* Washington, DC: Pew Hispanic Center.

Korzenny, F., and E. Schiff. 1987. Hispanic perceptions of communication discrimination. *Hispanic Journal of Behavioral Studies,* 9, 33–48.

Kravetz, C. 2006. *Latino identity.* McLean, VA: Association of Hispanic Advertising Agencies.

Magazine Publishers of America. 2004. *Hispanic/Latino market profile.* New York, NY: Magazine Publishers of America.

Marger, M. N. 1991. *Race and ethnic relations: American and global perspectives* (2nd ed.). Belmont, CA: Wadsworth.

Marín, G., and B. Van Oss Marín. 1991. *Research with Hispanic populations.* Applied Social Research Methods Series, 23. Thousand Oaks, CA: Sage Publications.

Media Report. 2006. Top advertisers in the Hispanic market. *Hispanic Business,* December.

National Center for Educational Statistics. 2005. *Public elementary and secondary students, staff, schools, and school districts: School year 2002–03.* NCES 2005–314. Washington, DC: NCES.

Osland, J. S., S. de Franco, and A. Osland. 1999. Organizational implications of Latin American culture: Lessons for the expatriate manager. *Journal of Management Inquiry* 8, no. 2: 219–234.

Padilla, A. 1980. The role of cultural awareness and ethnic loyalty in acculturation. In *Acculturation: Theory, models and some new findings,* ed. A. M. Padilla. Boulder, CO: Westview Press.

Passel, J. S. 2006. *Size and characteristics of unauthorized migrant population in the* U.S. Washington, DC: Pew Hispanic Center.

Pew Hispanic Center. October 10, 2006a. *From 200 million to 300 million: The numbers behind population growth.* Washington, DC: Pew Hispanic Center.

Pew Hispanic Center. 2006b. *Hispanics at mid-decade.* Washington, DC: Pew Hispanic Center.

Pew Hispanic Center. November 27, 2006c. *Latinos and the 2006 mid-term elections.* Washington, DC: Pew Hispanic Center.

Pew Hispanic Center and Kaiser Family Foundation. 2004. *2004 National survey of Latinos.* Washington, DC: Pew Hispanic Center

Ragins, B. R. 1989. Barriers to mentoring: The female manager's dilemma. *Human Relations, 42,* 1–22.

Ramírez, R. R., and G. P. de la Cruz. 2002. The Hispanic population in the United States: March 2002. *Current Populations Reports,* P20–P545. Washington, DC: U.S. Census Bureau.

Reich, M. H. 1986. The mentor collection. *Personnel* 63, no. 2: 50–56.

Reimers, C. W. 1992. Hispanic earnings and employment in the 1980s. In *Hispanics in the workplace,* ed. S. Knouse, P. Rosenfeld, and A. Culbertson, 29–55. Newbury Park, CA: Sage Publications.

Retirement Living Information Center. 2004. *Boomers seen redefining senior housing.* http://www.retirementliving.com/RLletterarchive_1204.html.

Rodriguez, R. 2004. Tapping the Hispanic labor pool. *HR Magazine* 49, no. 4: 72–79.

Rodriguez, R. 2005. Involving employees in leadership development. *Workforce Performance Solutions,* 1, no. 6 (June).

Rodriguez, R., 2006a. A CLO's role in future scenario planning. *Chief Learning Officer Magazine* 5, no. 1.

Rodriguez, R. 2006b. Creating an employment brand for your organization. *Workforce Performance Solutions* 2, no. 6: 36–50.

Rodriguez, R. 2006c. Diversity finds its place. *Human Resources Magazine* 51, no. 8: 56–61.

Salgado de Snyder, N .S., and V. Nelly. 1987. The role of ethnic loyalty among Mexican immigrant women. *Hispanic Journal of Behavioral Sciences* 9, no. 3: 287–298.

Schein, E. 2004. *Organizational culture and leadership.* New York: Jossey-Bass

Schoemaker, R. 2002. *Profiting from uncertainty: Strategies for succeeding no matter what brings.* New York: Simon & Schuster.

Sosa, L. 1999. *The Americano dream.* New York: Penguin Group.

Sosa, L. 2006. *Think and grow rich: A Latino choice.* New York: Ballantine Books.

Suro, R., M. Brodie, A. Steffenson, J. Valdes, and R. Levin. 2002. *2002 National survey of Latinos.* Washington, DC: Pew Hispanic Center.

Suro, R., and G. Escobar. 2006. *2006 National survey of Latinos: The immigration debate.* Washington, DC: Pew Hispanic Center.

Suro, R., and J. S. Passel. 2003. *The rise of the second generation: Changing patterns in Hispanic population growth.* Washington, DC: Pew Hispanic Center.

Synovate. 2004. *U.S. Hispanic market report.* Synovate Publications: www.synovate.com.

Tajfel, H., and J. C. Turner. 1986. The social identity theory of intergroup relations. In *Psychology of intergroup relations,* ed. S. Worchel and W. Austin, 7–24. Chicago: Nelson-Hall.

Tichy, N. 1998. *The leadership engine: Building leaders at every level.* Dallas, TX: Pritchett Publishing.

Triandis, H. C. 1985. *An Examination of Hispanic and general population perceptions of organizational environments: Final report to the Office of Naval Research.* Champaign: University of Illinois, Department of Psychology.

Triandis, H., C. Marín, J. Lisansky, and H. Betancourt. 1984. Simpatía as a cultural script of Hispanics. *Journal of Personality and Social Psychology* 47, no. 6: 1363–1375.

United States Hispanic Leadership Institute. *Almanac of Latino politics 2006.* Chicago, IL: U.S. Hispanic Leadership Institute.

Universum Communications. 2005. *Employer branding: Global best practices.* Philadelphia, PA: Universum Communications.

U.S. Census Bureau. 2000. *Census Bureau facts and figures.* CB00-FF. 11, September, 11.

U.S. Census Bureau. 2005. *Census Bureau facts and figures.* CB05-FF. 14–3, September 8.

U.S. Census Bureau, 2006a. 2002 *Survey of business owners: Hispanic owned firms.* CB06–41, March 21.

U.S. Census Bureau. 2006b. *Current population survey: 2005 Annual social and economic supplement,* October 26.

The U.S. Hispanic economy in transition: Facts, figures, and trends–2005. Santa Barbara, CA: *Hispanic Business,* April.

U.S. Small Business Administration. 2007. *Minorities in business: A demographic of minority business ownership.* Report 298, April 10.

Vara-Orta, F. 2007. Hispanic students pursue all cash, no loan philosophy. *Los Angeles Times,* February 11.

Vernon, S. W., and Roberts, R. E. 1985. A comparison of Anglos and Mexican Americans on selected measures of social support. *Hispanic Journal of Behavioral Sciences* 7, 381–399.

Index